Walking Away from Empire: A Personal Journey

Guy R. McPherson

PublishAmerica
Baltimore

D1444498

First printing

All characters in this book are fictitious, and any resemblance to real persons, living or dead, is coincidental.

PublishAmerica has allowed this work to remain exactly as the author intended, verbatim, without editorial input.

Softcover 978-1-4626-3887-1
PUBLISHED BY PUBLISHAMERICA, LLLP
www.publishamerica.com
Baltimore

Printed in the United States of America

For the remains of the living planet, and the humans who will
witness its comeback

Table of Contents

Introduction

My place of birth: the heart of the Aryan Nation, northern Idaho. The year: 1960. In so many ways, it was a time far different from today. The primary industries in the town of my birth were hard-rock mining and prostitution.

Ten years after my birth, living in a backwoods, redneck logging town even smaller than the town in which I was born, I'm walking along a gravel road on my way to elementary school. I look up to see a 13-year-old student pointing a rifle out his bedroom window. It was aimed at my head. I knew better than to run. If I showed fear, he might shoot. We can't outrun bullets. The incident was so ordinary I didn't bother to tell my parents for another two decades. It just never came up. America's Cultural Revolution spread its messages of tolerance and free love to northern Idaho long after it rippled through the rest of the nation.

As a 6'1", 165-pound, ripped 18-year-old, I could work or play all day without a break. As was typical for male athletes in my small town, I was recruited by the Idaho Department of Lands to fight wildfires. I held the position for five summers while attending college, thriving on the adrenaline of chasing smoke via truck or helicopter. During my second season as a smokechaser, believing myself an immortal 19-year-old with the world firmly under my control, I stumbled upon a large, informative wildfire.

Because it was lunchtime and most of the crew was unavailable, I made the initial attack myself. I drove an hour in a small four-wheel-drive truck with 300 gallons of water, and then walked ten minutes in the direction of the billowing column of smoke. I nearly stepped on a rattlesnake en route, but I barely broke stride in beheading it with a single swat of my shovel. Topping a hill with the shovel, a radio, and a quart of water, I saw the flames dancing through the underbrush and then leaping into the crowns of the trees overhead. One glance taught me an important lesson: Some natural phenomena are beyond human control. I called in aircraft with loads of fire retardant, pumper trucks with more firefighters, and a helicopter to manage the assault.

Ultimately, we put out the fire. Actually, the weather had a lot more to do with suppressing the fire than did the dozens of firefighters and state-of-the-art equipment. The fire hardened my resolve to study fire ecology, a topic I pursued through graduate school and a post-doctoral program before broadening my ecological horizons. As an ecologist, I studied limits to growth, interconnections between components of ecosystems, and the reliance of humans on Earth. Nonetheless, my early efforts at teaching, scholarship, and outreach were well within culture's main stream. Indeed, between the fire's shocking lesson -- which came after the exam, the literal trial by fire -- until the decade of my forties, I rarely looked up from the miniscule to the larger world, much less questioned the system in which I was ensconced. I was successful by every imperial measure: I was well-published in all the right places, my students acquired the best jobs in the field, and the professional service I provided was exemplary. I earned enough to live on a third of my income and still traveled as much as I desired throughout the industrialized world.

In other words, I was the perfect model of all that is wrong with the United States and, by extension, the nations looking to us as a model. Rather than questioning the system, I was raising minor questions within the system.

During the decade of my forties, I transformed my academic life from mainstream ecologist to friend of the earth. I became a conservation biologist and social critic, and my speaking and writing increasingly targeted the public beyond the classroom. At the request of a woman who was to become a dear friend, I began teaching poetry in jail and juvey hall, trying to give voice to wise people long marginalized or ignored by industrial society. My guest commentaries in local newspapers pointed out the absurdities of American life, as well as limits to growth for the world's industrial economy. My increasingly strident essays drew the attention of university administrators who tried to fire me, and, when that failed, tried to muzzle me. But they found both routes too difficult to impinge upon a tenured full professor. Shortly after they gave up trying to force my departure, I left the institution on my own terms in dismay and disgust.

A circuitous and invigorating journey took me from benighted village to the ivory tower, from naïve country bumpkin to public intellectual. In many ways emblematic of tail-end Baby Boomers, I witnessed massive changes in our attitudes about environmental protection and social justice during America's turbulent Cultural Revolution. A product of western civilization and its ultimate expression, industrial culture, I came of age during the peak of U.S. power. For the initial three decades of my life, I took advantage of the atypically high standard of living in the United States without questioning what allowed us such indulgence. More recently, as I have become more knowledgeable and therefore more guilt-ridden about the tremendous oppression this country visits abroad, and the similarly tremendous obedience we require at home, I have taken a decidedly non-mainstream path. In the wake of considerable angst, I've tried to opt out of western civilization.

Abandoning industrial culture in a globalized world is no mean feat. Because sucking guts out of bugs in one of the few remaining regions still isolated from western civilization holds little appeal to me, I have returned to my rural roots. At the age of 49 and at the height of my productive career, I leapt out of the ivory tower to live as part *of* the world, rather than apart *from* the world. This collection of essays reveals a small portion of my thoughts and feelings as I leave the suburban culture of make believe to pursue the good life, surrounded by the natural world and rooted in a new human community.

These deeply personal essays explore the fertile ground at the largely unplowed intersection of conservation biology and philosophy, an intersection I addressed superficially and poorly in an earlier book, *Killing the Natives: Has the American Dream Become a Nightmare?* The most frequent topics in this domain are also the topics I believe to be the most important subjects in the history of humanity: the twin sides of the fossil-fuel coin. Energy decline, commonly known as "peak oil," will derail growth of the industrial economy, ultimately bringing us closer to Earth and our neighbors. Whether there is world enough, and time, to save the remaining remnants of the living planet remains to be seen. After all, the other side of the fossil-fuel coin rises like a horrifying specter on the horizon: Global climate change poses a significant threat to every species on the planet, including *Homo sapiens*.

In addition to conservation of the living planet and the associated drivers, these essays also dabble in the realms of art, literature, C.P. Snow's eponymous *Two Cultures*, and academia. I'd like to think that, like Walt Whitman, I am large; I contain multitudes.

I call myself a conservation biologist, yet I did not discover the enterprise of conservation biology, much less become a conservation biologist, until long after my formal education was complete. My undergraduate curriculum in forestry and my graduate programs in range science were tilted heavily toward extraction of natural resources. Like most people, I believed the world was here for human use. My focus on extraction was not the only obstacle between me and the pursuit of conservation biology. The greater challenge was that the field of conservation biology, as exemplified by publication of the first issue of *Conservation Biology*, emerged the same year I was granted a Ph.D. Thus, there were no formal university courses in conservation biology until my days on the student side of the classroom were behind me. My own laser-like focus on applied ecology prevented me noticing the field for a full decade after it appeared on the American scene, although I now call myself a conservation biologist. In doing so, I recognize that my credentials are suspect. But if my hypocrisy reveals false credentials, it also verifies my membership into the club known as *Homo sapiens*.

In contrast to my claim to be a conservation biologist, I make no claim to being a philosopher in any formal manner. Through high school and nine years of higher education culminating in a doctoral degree, I did not attempt a single course in philosophy. I was exposed briefly, superficially, and vicariously to a dab of Karl Popper and perhaps another philosopher or two who subsequently escapes my long-term memory. And yet I earned a Doctor of Philosophy in that least philosophical of majors, range science (in my days as a graduate student the field centered largely on production of red meat; apparently it continues to do so, without admitting as much). I discovered Socrates very late in an unexamined life. In my defense, I have been working hard in recent years to fill the philosophical void (not to mention the existential one).

Contrary to my dubious credentials as a conservation biologist and philosopher, I have complete confidence in my knowledge of ecology. I have been thoroughly educated about the importance of limits to growth with respect to individuals and societies, and my scholarship on global climate change and energy decline merely reflect a rich ecological tradition. Furthermore, any reasonably literate observer would be hard pressed to ignore the expansive evidence on contemporary industrialized societies of global climate change or peak oil. In my opinion, the intellectual absorption of this evidence should push us, admittedly one at a time, toward additional understanding of philosophy. Like that ten-year-old boy of more than four decades ago, in terms of planetary survival we now all have a gun pointed at our heads. There is no way to outrun the bullets. This is no time to panic, no time to run. It's time to face reality without showing fear.

REASON

The choices we face

At this late juncture in the era of industry, it seems safe to assume we face one of two futures. If we continue to burn fossil fuels, we face imminent environmental collapse. If we cease burning fossil fuels, the industrial economy will collapse. Industrial humans express these futures as a choice between your money or your life, and tell you that, without money, life isn't worth living. As should be clear by now, industrial humans -- or at least our "leaders" -- have chosen not door number one (environmental collapse) and not door number two (economic collapse), but *both of the above.*

If you believe your life depends upon water coming out the taps and food showing up at the grocery store, you'll defend to the death the system that keeps water coming out the taps and food showing up at the grocery story. News flash: If you think your life depends on that system, you're a very unusual human, especially historically, and you support an unusual culture marked by overwhelming collateral damage to non-industrial cultures and non-human species. And you're sorely mistaken, besides.

The predicament we face is environmental overshoot, as a handful of ecologists have been saying for decades (thereby echoing Malthus). We've far exceeded the human carrying capacity of the planet. As a result, we threaten most of the species on Earth, including our own, with extinction by the end of this century. Currently, there is not nearly enough food to feed every human on the planet, even at the expense of nearly every non-human species. Actually, tens of thousands of people have been starving to death every day for a few decades, but they've been hidden beyond our imperial television screens.

The root cause of the problem is complex, but it can be reduced to a few primary factors: agriculture (i.e., western culture), industrialization (the epitome of western civilization), and their contribution to human population growth. The genus *Homo* persisted on the planet some 2 million years, and our own species had been around for at least 250,000 years, without exceeding carrying capacity. We actually lived without posing a threat to the persistence of other species. During those years -- two million of them, in fact -- humans had abundant spare time for socializing and art, and spent only a few hours each week hunting, gathering, and otherwise feeding themselves (i.e., "working"). Contrast those conditions with today's humans, and how much time we spend working (and rarely enjoying that work, if talk around the water cooler is any indication). Agriculture leads to food storage, which leads to empire, which produces slavery, oppression, and mass murder (all of which were essentially absent for the first couple million years of the *Homo* experience). Lives were relatively short, but happy by every measure we can find. In short, without agriculture there is no environmental overshoot. The human population explosion is effect, not cause. The industrial revolution exacerbated the problem to such an extent we'll never be able to recover without historic human suffering. We are only beginning to witness the impacts of reduced energy supplies on the industrial economy, and we'll be squarely in the post-industrial Stone Age, fully unprepared, within two decades at most.

At this point, our commitment to western culture (i.e., civilization) is so great that any attempt to power down will result in suffering and death of millions (and probably billions). Nonetheless, it's the only way to allow our own species, and millions of others, to persist beyond century's end and squeeze through the global-change bottleneck (which, as we know, resulted from industrialization). Every day in overshoot is another day to be reckoned with later, and therefore another few thousand humans who must live and die in Hobbesian fashion. There are no decent solutions. A collapse in the world's industrial economy is producing the expected results, finally, too late to save thousands of species we've sent into the abyss, but perhaps barely in time to save a few remaining species, including our own. If you care about other species and cultures, or even the continued persistence of our own species, then an impressive body of evidence suggests you support our imminent transition to the post-industrial Stone Age. Such a trip saves the maximum number of human lives, over the long term.

When you realize the (eco)systems in the real world actually produce your food and water, you'll defend to the death the systems that produces your food and water. I'm in that camp. How about you? What do you support? The industrial culture of death, which sanctions murderous actions every day? Or the culture of life?

Philosophy and conservation

Asking a contemporary scientist in possession of a Ph.D. (i.e., a Doctor of Philosophy degree) any question about philosophy typically draws a blank stare or, occasionally, an inquisitive gaze. Philosophy rarely is taught in science classes at any level of education, including the Ph.D. Across campus, a dose of science is taught in the philosophy department, but practicing scientists rarely are involved in the conversation.

Yet the identical twins Science and Philosophy were born in ancient Athens. Most contemporary philosophers claim the twins' father was Thales of Miletus (a city in Asia Minor, now Turkey), largely based on two events: Thales was the first to calculate the height of Egypt's pyramids (which he did before traveling to Greece, by measuring the length of the pyramids' shadows) and, even more notably, the first to predict a solar eclipse (in 585 BC). Inseparable and indistinguishable for nearly two millennia, Science and Philosophy were viewed as one and the same child. Little evidence remains of Thales, and the majority of his ideas ultimately were buried beneath the landslide of Grecian reason capped by Socrates and Plato. Philosophical advances continued to pile up, but Alfred North Whitehead famously described two millennia of these advances as mere footnotes to Plato.

Despite minor quibbles, Science and Philosophy remained close for several centuries before they were irrevocably forced apart during, ironically, the Enlightenment. Although most educated people could distinguish the twins by the mid-1600s, when intellectual and political battles produced notable differences in the twin icons of reason, they remained friends for another three centuries, until the biblical root of all evil came between them. By 1945, Bertrand Russell introduced his comprehensive *History of Western Philosophy* by dividing knowledge into three categories: science represents the known universe, theology represents dogma (which I would not call "knowledge"), and philosophy represents the "No Man's Land" between the two. Russell concluded that philosophy, like science, relies on reason and that, like theology, it consists of speculations beyond definitive knowledge. Scientific advances resulting from the Enlightenment reduced philosophy to such a narrow domain that it "suffered more from modernity than any other field of human endeavor," according to Hannah Arendt's 1958 book, *The Human Condition* (p. 294). The post-Aristotle shift from deduction to induction contributed to, or perhaps merely was symptomatic of, philosophy's demise and the coincident rise of science.

In the wake of World War II and five years after Russell's capacious historical account acknowledged and contributed to the chasm between science and philosophy, Franklin D. Roosevelt signed the legislation that created the National Science Foundation of the United States (NSF). This new and influential organization swung the final ax that doomed Science and Philosophy to separate existences. The NSF was created in 1950 and became a dominant influence -- perhaps *the* dominant influence -- on the nature and conduct of science by 1955. Confined to separate quarters, Science and Philosophy barely speak to each other in the 21st century. Casual observers would never know they once looked alike, as evidenced by treatment of the two entities on university campuses: compartmentalization is the order of the day.

The marginalization of philosophy has coincided with the rise of "big science." British philosopher John Gray goes so far as to write (in his excellent short book, *Straw Dogs: Thoughts on Humans and Other Animals*), "philosophy is a subject without a subject matter" (p. 82).

Well, maybe. I tend to think of philosophy in much the same way I think about science and art: it's personal. Paul Feyerabend's dogmatic postmodernism notwithstanding, science has rules, more or less. But science as a way of understanding the universe -- in sharp contrast to the societal expectation of science as a never-ending font of technology -- is a personal journey of curiosity addressed with unbridled creativity. So, too, are art and philosophy. Although science often produces knowledge that is more repeatable and reliable than the other two endeavors, it's not at all clear that either outcome is used by, or useful for, the typical person. On the other hand, many people use technology – the (incorrectly) perceived point of science -- as a tool to assault the natural world while temporarily satisfying our insatiable urge to divorce ourselves from physical reality. Whether the divorce is intentional or not is beyond the scope of my knowledge and this text.

If reason arose in Athens, passion for the natural world was born in the Orient. Specifically, Lao Tzu's masterful book of poetry *Tao Te Ching* was written approximately coincident with the development of pre-Socratic philosophy in Greece (the birth year of Lao Tzu, who represented a single person or a conglomeration of identities, traditionally is accepted as 570 BC, 15 years after Thales predicted a solar eclipse). Whereas Platonists often are blamed for divorcing humanity from the natural world, Eastern thought has maintained a tight connection between humans and their environment, and has exalted nature in the process (China's recent embrace of free-market capitalism has produced the expected deterioration of that country's environment). *Tao Te Ching* is the most famous example in the Western world, but Lao Tzu merely was reflecting his culture. (Consider chapter 33: "Knowing others is wisdom; Knowing the self is enlightenment. / Mastering others requires force; Mastering the self requires strength; He who knows he has enough is rich. / Perseverance is a sign of will power. / He who stays where he is endures. / To die but not to perish is to be eternally present.") Further, cursory inspection of virtually any of the major Eastern religions reveals strong links between nature and humanity.

Reason arose in Greece about 25 centuries ago, and is perhaps best known from Plato's *Socratic Dialogues*. Plato (ca. 428-348 BC) uses the conversations of Socrates to pose and explore questions in considerable detail. Although many of the issues and associated conversations seem unsophisticated to contemporary readers, these initial attempts to employ logic to study the natural world and the role of humans in the world are remarkable precisely because they were unprecedented. The contributions of ancient Greece to the material worldview that characterizes modernity cannot be overstated; that so many of the contributions came from Athens, a city that never exceeded 250,000 residents, is simply astonishing.

Although the ancient Greeks laid the foundation for modernity, few bricks were added to the structure for nearly two millennia. During the early seventeenth century, the empiricist Francis Bacon (1561-1626) and the deconstructionist Rene Descartes (1596-1650) ushered in the Enlightenment, thereby triggering a flurry of construction to the edifice of knowledge. Almost overnight it became clear that the world was a material one that could be observed and quantified by all who dared think and observe. Nature obeyed rules and humans were big-brained animals capable of discovering and describing those rules.

Thus, the Enlightenment eroded the role of authority as a source of knowledge. In the wake of Giordano Bruno's heinous execution by the Catholic Church, Galileo recanted earlier statements in which he denied the Ptolemaic view that Earth was the center of the universe. But the erosion of authority that began as a trickle quickly became a flood, and the Church was increasingly marginalized as a source of knowledge.

David Hume (1711-1776), in his initial written piece of philosophy, presented a compelling case against miracles, hence against religion: "Of Miracles" was published in 1748 as an essay in *An Enquiry Concerning Human Understandings*. (Hume became particularly well known the idea that what "is" does not indicate what "ought" to be.) Shortly before Charles Darwin formalized the theory of evolution by natural selection in the *Origin of Species* (1859), Schopenhauer (1788-1860) used Plato-like dialogue to question the basis of religion ("Religion: A Dialogue") and Max Stirner declared the death of God in his 1845 book, *The Ego and Its Own*. Notably influenced by Schopenhauer and writing shortly after publication of Darwin's dangerous idea, Friedrich Nietzsche (1844-1900) vociferously spread the word about God's death (probably without awareness of Stirner's work) while predicting that Reason would overwhelm worldviews based on mysticism (while proclaiming science to be a lie; like all other humans, Hume and Nietzsche contained many contradictions). Nietzsche expressed his views on Christianity early and often in his writings, most popularly with *Thus Spoke Zarathustra*. I prefer *The Antichrist* because it represents Nietzsche's views on God particularly clearly and vehemently. And also because this work was intended to be shockingly blasphemous.

With respect to the rise of Reason, Nietzsche was an optimist. As S. Jonathan Singer concludes in his 2001 book, *The Splendid Feast of Reason*, it appears unlikely that more than ten percent of people are capable of employing reason as a basis for how they live. Singer likely did not know he was echoing Schopenhauer, although Schopenhauer's use of dialogue in his essay clearly indicates he knew he was echoing Plato in reaching the same conclusion.

Collectively, these voices from the Enlightenment illustrate the capacity for, and importance of, Reason. Reason is the basis for understanding the material world. As such, it serves as the foundation upon which conservation biology, nature-human interactions, and durable living in human communities can be understood and practiced. We can willingly conserve nature and its parts only through description and understanding rooted in reality. Mysticism has proven an insufficient foundation for conserving nature. Ultimately, it doubtless will prove inadequate for saving humanity as well.

It is not at all clear that humankind can be saved (or, for that matter, is worth saving). Evolution drives us to survive, drives us to procreate, and drives us to accumulate material possessions. Evolution always pushes us toward the brink, and culture piles on, hurling us into the abyss. Nietzsche was correct about our lack of free will -- as Gray points out in *Straw Dogs* -- free will is an illusion. It's not merely the foam on the beer: it's the last bubble of foam, the one that just popped. It's no surprise, then, that we are sleepwalking into the future, or that the future is a formidably tall cliff.

Creating faith

Not so long ago, humans believed the watershed was everything. Their world was restricted to a tiny area, and traveling beyond the area was undesirable and often dangerous. But some daring traveler took the leap and discovered a world beyond the watershed.

Rinse and repeat, from the watershed to the continent, from the continent to the world, from the world to the solar system, from the solar system to the galaxy, from the galaxy to the universe. If the Church hadn't killed a few daring travelers along the way, we'd have discovered a lot more a lot sooner. Call it the collateral damage of controlling the empire.

Human discovery represents a continuum, with our part diminishing along the way. The world was large, but we were large, too. Geographical discoveries and our ability to travel made the world smaller. And then the solar system, and so on, so that now we've explained the universe in physical terms and we understand our inconsequential role (and our hubris, which is quite consequential).

Religious believers like to believe we're special, that Somebody is watching over us. And they use the most stunning logic to explain the notion of Somebody: Science only explains our universe back to the Big Bang. What about before then? And what caused the Bang, and all the matter associated with it? It must have come from something. By which they mean Somebody.

As if pointing to Somebody explains it all.

Stephen B. Hawking tried to explain the idea of a singularity to the lay public in his dreadfully incomprehensible 1988 book, *A Brief History of Time*, undoubtedly one of the most-purchased, least-read books of all time. Needless to say, Hawking's prose failed to provide an explanation convincing to the masses. But here's the bottom line: Universes come and go, and they collapse and arise in events called singularities.

Fast-forward to the Russian physicist Alex Vilenkin and his 2006 book, *Many Worlds in One*. Vilenkin explains that ours is one of many universes -- an infinite number, in fact. If you buy the evidence behind an expanding universe (which is overwhelming), then it's a short, simple, and logical step to ours being one of an infinite number of universes. We're part of the multiverse. The continuum rolls on.

Most universes likely blink out as quickly as they arise. They persist only a few nanoseconds, and fail to produce even a single flower. Some of these universes, such as ours, are relatively stable. They persist long enough, and have sufficient initial conditions, to support the development of life. If they are stable long enough, so-called intelligent life arises. Count up all these universes, come to terms with the concept of infinity, and you've got an infinite number of Guy McPhersons typing these words now.

This explanation accounts for all matter, and all energy, for all universes, for all time. Thus, it explains our universe, and the universes that preceded ours, and so on, back to infinity ago (and also from now until infinity).

Many of you are thinking, "Yeah, but what about before that?" If you want to know what came before infinity, then you don't understand infinity.

Since the brains of most of us are somewhat smaller than infinity, religious believers will never admit that physical processes might explain more about the universe -- or even the multiverse -- than that "explanation" to trump all explanations, "Somebody did it." Somebody big and mysterious that we'll never understand: Somebody like Gawd, Yahweh, the Great Spirit, or the unicorn on the dark side of the moon. But invoking Somebody is choosing to remain ignorant or -- and I suspect this is the customary route -- not thinking about one's own personal system of beliefs. The former is a personal choice, of course, and I'm happy to let religious believers keep believing instead of thinking. Especially if they let me think. It'd be even better if they encouraged their children to think, but I realize that's asking a lot.

It's pretty demoralizing to think there are an infinite number of Earths dealing with peak oil and runaway greenhouse by promoting destruction and ignorance. But it's pretty cool to think that there are an infinite number of planet Earths that produced humans with empathy, compassion, and creativity. On these Earths, humans persist a very long time and humbly share the planet with many other species. On

24

these Earths, there is no runaway greenhouse. Passing the planetary oil peak is cause for celebration because, on these Earths, the demise of cheap oil doesn't spell the end of planetary destruction via civilization, much less the likely demise of a majority of the humans on Earth.

Reason's tortuous path

Reason is the basis for understanding the material world. Mysticism has proven an insufficient foundation for dealing with energy decline and runaway greenhouse. As such, I suspect it will prove inadequate for saving humanity. Whether or not we're worth saving is a separate issue.

The pursuit of truth is not always fun, of course. Popular culture and its cousin, organized religion, constantly impede the quest of knowledge and search for wisdom. I am reminded of the Catholic Church's treatment of my long-time hero, Giordano Bruno, which gave Galileo reason to recant in the face of astronomical truth. Trapped and captured by the Inquisition, Bruno was periodically interrogated during eight years of torture-laden imprisonment. Refusing to abandon the Copernican view that Earth orbits the sun instead of the converse Aristotelean (and, more importantly at the time, Catholic) view, Bruno was tongue-tied (literally) and burned alive in February of 1600. Legend, which is seldom true but which nicely embellishes a good story, has him spending his last words assailing the Church because its fear of the truth exceeded his fear of death.

Copernicus, Bruno, and Galileo were right, of course, as the Church admitted a scant 392 years after murdering Bruno. In a remarkable demonstration of how quickly the Church is capable of admitting its errors and catching up to scientific facts, it concluded Charles Darwin was right about evolution only a couple years later. Perhaps in another few years they will admit the Jesus-as-prophet craze was just a joke that got out of hand, or, more outrageously, they will begin asking their practitioners to follow Jesus' teachings.

Unfortunately, the Church does not reward those who speak the truth today nearly as publicly as it once persecuted them, and it does not preach scientific truth nearly as vociferously as it preaches mindless mysticism. Periodic condemnation of Darwin by priests and bishops suggests that the Church is slow to educate its own leaders and that it tolerates some facts more willingly than others. But enough, for now, about the Catholic Church, which is too easy a target for those who purposely invoke reason, a much more powerful force in politics and religion than the Catholic Church. Furthermore, the Church's fundamentalist Protestant descendants are making even the Catholic Church seem sensible of late.

I don't mind the precepts of religion, even though religions are founded on an idea for which there is no evidence. What I mind is religious adherents living contrary to their prophets. I would be a big fan of Christianity if Christians lived as Jesus did, or as he instructed them to live (e.g., forgoing the pursuit of material possessions in the name of a life of service, and stewarding Earth instead of abusing it). As Nietzsche pointed out in *The Antichrist*, there was one Christian. And he died on the cross.

With respect to reason, our challenge may be far greater than I once imagined. I would not be the first to suggest that, just as a minority of people is incapable of distinguishing colors that are obvious to the majority, a majority is unable to differentiate between reasonable arguments and specious ones. Singer makes perhaps the strongest argument for this case in *The Splendid Feast of Reason*. The evidence he reviews demonstrates that rational people have not comprised a majority of any society, suggesting that rational thought lies beyond the realm of most humans. He further concludes that such "rationalists," as he calls them, comprise fewer than ten percent of American society. Mind you, this is not about intelligence: Plenty of people who are very intelligent (by any measure) are unable to allow logic and reason to overcome irrationality. Thus, contrary to the belief and expectation of Bacon and Descartes, it would appear that efforts to unlock nature's secrets and then pass along this knowledge have become a lost cause. Indeed, "lost" may be the wrong term for it: Perhaps most people simply cannot receive and interpret the language of reason. If this is the case, as increasing evidence purports, it should be no surprise that history has treated badly the few rational people bold enough to take a firm stand in the face of an irrational majority.

The rational minority often is treated as irrational, making me wonder if assuming a rational stance is, in fact, as irrational as it is abnormal. This appears to be classic case of the inmates running the asylum, and proclaiming one's sanity is a one-way ticket to solitary confinement (from which, to begin with, rationalists are only one step removed). The impressive swiftness with which the majority has persecuted vocal proponents of reason provides plenty of cause for reflection and even retraction, which was the path taken by Galileo when faced with Bruno's fate. The title of Singer's book is well chosen, for it glorifies reason while acknowledging the rarity of its application.

A fundamental question thus becomes: Is the inability of most people to employ reason sufficient justification to cast aside the quest for truth? What about to deny the truth? Why should we try to teach the irrational majority? Why not continue the quest for truth, enjoy the company of the rational ten percent, and leave the masses to their apparently inherent ignorance? Contrast the choices of Galileo and Bruno. Some causes are worth dying for, even though the number of Martin Luthers pales in comparison to the virtual unknowns such as Giordano Bruno.

Singer proposes science as the solution. I'd like to believe science would succeed where reason has failed, but it is difficult to maintain optimism. After all, science gave us evolution by natural selection, and overwhelming evidence has subsequently reinforced Charles Darwin's dangerous idea. Yet the American public cannot grasp the notion, with denial of the rudimentary science-based facts consistently running at seventy-five percent (among industrialized nations on this topic, none come close to American ignorance and denial of the facts).

But it appears we have no viable choice. If reason is not the answer, then Renaissance and the associated Enlightenment were temporary diversions along the path of absurdity, and Giordano Bruno died in vain. I cannot accept mysticism as a legitimate alternative to rational thought any more than a philosopher can accept superficial thinking or a musician can tolerate improper pitch. I cannot surrender to the dual forces of ignorance and denial, though I recognize their great power.

The connection between reason and daily life grows ever more tenuous as the empire crumbles, and there's nothing quite like Christmas in this "Christian" nation. Christianity's most holy days encourage disassociation from reality in a culture already largely devoid of real-world experiences. The ability of believers to suspend disbelief, to rely on faith instead of evidence, is damned impressive. And it extends well beyond the supernatural. Once you take Kierkegaard's "leap of faith," it's a small step to believe in the benevolence of Empire. Surely gawd won't stop taking care of the chosen people of the United States.

Or will she?

Recently I received a Christmas card that was unintentionally soaked in irony. I'll skip the rant about celebrating Christ and mass, the two components of Christ's mass (i.e., Christmas) in which I don't believe, much less celebrate. And, too, Ill forgo the equally tempting rant about a religious holiday that promotes conspicuous consumption in an empire founded on secular ideals.

On to that card: It was filled with proud stories of the kids in the U.S. Army, and it closed with, "We pray for peace." I don't know whether to laugh or cry.

Never mind that the writer almost certainly is fooling herself. If her prayers are answered, that'll put the battle-ready kids out of their jobs. And, since war comprises the foundation for our entire industrial economy, the empire almost surely would sink to the bottom of the already stinking swamp within weeks of an outbreak of peace. Praying for peace makes as much sense as supporting the troops, and both cases of wishful thinking are clothed in lies.

I realized how offensive most people find my view. And yet, I can't seem to stop myself. Any decent social critic points out the lunacy of societal taboos. I'm not suggesting I'm a decent social critic. But I can no longer ignore this most annoying of taboos.

Support the troops. It's the rallying cry of an entire nation. It's the slogan pasted on half the bumpers in the country.

Supporting the troops is pledging your support for the empire. Supporting the troops supports the occupation of sovereign nations because might makes right. Supporting the troops supports wanton murder of women and children throughout the world. And men, too. Supporting the troops supports obedience at home and oppression abroad. Supporting the troops throws away every ideal on which this country allegedly is founded. Supporting the troops supports the ongoing destruction of the living planet in the name of economic growth. Supporting the troops therefore hastens our extinction in exchange for a few dollars. Supporting the troops means caving in to Woodrow Wilson's neo-liberal agenda, albeit cloaked as contemporary neo-conservatism (cf. hope and change). Supporting the troops trumpets power as freedom and fascism as democracy.

Perhaps most importantly, supporting the troops means giving up on resistance. Resistance is all we have, and all we've ever had. We say we're mad as hell and we claim we're not going to take it any more. But, sadly, we gave up on resistance of any kind years ago. After all, we might get in trouble. We might be incarcerated for protesting without a permit.

When jets from the nearby military base scream over the university campus, conversation stops, indoors or out. We pause awkwardly, stopped in mid-conversation. After the jets pass, in formation, an excuse often is articulated by the person with whom I'm visiting: "It's the sound of freedom."

My response never varies: "Sounds like oppression to me."

The ensuing silence is more awkward than the scream of the jet engines.

It's as if America's cultural revolution never happened. It's as if we never questioned the dominant paradigm in an empire run amok, as if we never experienced Woodstock and the Summer of Love, bra-burning hippies and war-torn teenagers, Rosa Parks and the Cuyahoga River. We're right back in the 1950s, swimming in culture's main stream instead of questioning, resisting, and protesting.

In a Tucson coffee shop in mid-2011 I saw a woman, apparently in her early twenties, dressed in a short skirt, an apron, and high heels. Had she been behind the counter, she would have been the perfect symbol of the 1950s, a refugee from two generations gone by. We've moved from the unquestioning automatons of Aldous Huxley and George Orwell to the firebrands of a radical counter-cultural worldview and back again. A generational sea change swept us from post-war "liberators" drunk on early 1950s propaganda to revolutionaries willing to take risks in defense of late 1960s ideals. The revolution gained steam through the 1970s, but lost its way when the U.S. industrial economy hit the speed bump of domestic peak oil. The Carter Doctrine -- the world's oil belongs to us -- coupled with Ronald Reagan's soothing pack of lies, was the perfect match to our middle-aged comfort, so we abandoned the noble ideals of earlier days for another dose of palliative propaganda. Three decades later, we've swallowed so much Soma we wouldn't couldn't find a hint of revolution in Karl Marx's *Communist Manifesto*.

In short, the pillars of social justice and environmental protection rose from the cesspool of ignorance to become shining lights for an entire generation. And then we let them fall back into the swamp. The very notion that others matter -- much less that those others are worth fighting for -- has been relegated to the dustbin of history.

The problem with being a martyr: You have to die for the cause. And along the way, you'll probably be jailed and tortured. But there's a fate far worse than being a martyr, in the minds of America's youth. There's the thought you'll be viewed as an anti-American freak, out of touch with Lady Gaga and *Dancing With The Stars*. A fate worse than death: Your Facebook page will be removed, thus "disappearing" you.

A line from Eugene Debs, five-time candidate of the Socialist party for U.S. president, comes to mind: "While there is a lower class I am in it, while there is a criminal element I am of it; while there is a soul in prison, I am not free." He was serious. So am I. That I am not taken seriously in these most serious of days pulverizes my ego. That Debs is not taken seriously these days shatters my heart.

When I visit with college-age people these days, they have no idea what I mean, and they believe Debs and I are misguided jokers. Completely immersed in a culture of make believe, mind-fucked from birth by the corporations running the media, the thought of resistance is, quite simply, beyond the pale. Resistance? Against what? And why? Isn't resistance a form of terrorism?

Every revolution has failed. And if that's not sufficient reason to launch a revolution, I don't know what is. The revolution is dead: Viva la revolution!

If any one of those troops we claim to support attempts to bring transparency and reform to this country, we instantly turn on him and support his torture by -- you guessed it -- the troops. And who's the commander in chief of these troops? That's right, the man who promised transparency and reform, but who now seeks to crush the very people trying to bring it to us. The case of Bradley Manning comes immediately to mind, though it's hardly a solitary example.

If obliterating transparency means criminalizing journalism, we can live with that. Those journalists are probably terrorists anyway. Or worse, liberals. The First Amendment was shredded by Obama's predecessor, and how it's being turned to ash. The U.S. Constitution and Bill of Rights are bobbing along the same waves as social justice and environmental protection, sold down the river by a nation addicted to growth for the sake of growth (the ideology of a cancer cell).

It seems very little matters to the typical American beyond economic growth. And for that, most importantly, we need an uninterrupted supply of crude oil. All wars are resource wars, and even our involvement in the last "Good War" was about oil, notwithstanding revisionist history about our compassion regarding Hitler's final solution. Crude oil's near-term annual decline rate of ten percent means many troops will be needed to secure the lifeblood of the industrial economy. After all, world demand hasn't peaked yet, although world supply has. If we're to continue ruining the world, we'll need plenty of troops. And they'll need your support.

You keep supporting the troops, and trying to convince yourself you're fighting terrorism in the process. If doubt creeps in, turn on the television. Listen to the news anchors and the politicians, the characters, and the commercials. Immerse yourself in the ultimate hallucination. Keep lapping up the self-censored "news," confident the future will bring even more self-indulgent hedonism than the recent past.

And if somebody tries to tell you the hegemony of the U.S. dollar is threatened, thereby causing the price of oil to skyrocket, you just ignore the uncomfortable news, just as the mainstream media have ignored it. That kind of thing can't happen here. It's never happened, so it can't happen (Francis Bacon's *Idol of the Den*). If some misinformed fool attempts to point out the consequences of consumerism, shrug him off as a terrorist. And if somebody tries to confuse your happy holidays by telling you the good news about economic collapse, you tell him you'll be praying for peace. That'll make it all okay.

Some of these ideas first appeared in my 2006 book, *Letters to a Young Academic: Seeking Teachable Moments*.

Math: the scary kind, not the fuzzy kind

A little rudimentary math indicates we're using oil at the rate of about 5,500 cubic feet per second (cfs). As any river-runner knows, that's quite a bit of flow.

Thirteen times during the 80 years of record, the perennial river out my window, which is the last free-flowing river in the state of New Mexico, has exceeded 5,500 cfs. Several days of unremitting rain gets it flowing to 3,000 cfs, which is more than enough for an exciting ride via canoe, kayak, or rubber raft. And it's about half the current flow of oil.

That's simply staggering.

Here's another shot of perspective: We burn a cubic mile of crude oil every year. The Empire State Building, the world's ninth-tallest building, towers above New York at 1,250 feet. The world's tallest building, Taipei 101, is 1,667 feet from ground to tip. Put those buildings together, end to end, and you have one side of a cube. Do it again, and you have the second side. Once more, but this time straight up, and you have one big cube. Filling that cube with oil takes nearly 200 billion gallons, which is about one-sixth the size of the cube of oil we're burning every year.

Sorry for the redundancy, but that's simply staggering.

I'm starting to understand the many peak-oil deniers out there. It's tough to wrap our hummingbird-sized intellects around these pterodactyl-sized numbers. Our ability to power down with all the peace and tranquility of Buddhist monks seems a little far-fetched (we are, as pointed out by Nietzsche, "all too human"). It's easier to deny the impending collapse of empire than to deal with facts.

Ultimately, we'll be forced to face reality. Soon enough, we'll be using less oil. A lot less, I'd guess, and sooner than most people think. Such are the consequences of the end of American Empire and the closely related industrial economy of the globe.

Many things could accelerate the fall of American Empire. Leaders at all levels of government are working on most of them. They are joined by leaders of corporations and most non-profit organizations, stuffed full of themselves and "knowledge" about leadership. They generate bullshit at about 3,000 cfs. That's a lot, but it's not keeping up with the lifeblood of empire.

Fortunately for Earth and the species thereon, including *Homo sapiens*, we have passed well beyond the world peak in crude oil extraction and therefore moved beyond the age of inexpensive oil. But what are the causes and consequences of expensive oil? We know there is a strongly negative relationship between the price of oil and economic growth, and we know supply is constrained at this point (but the constraint is manifest largely in "third-world" countries).

Here in the homeland, we passed peak in 1970 and we extract relatively little oil on land or at sea. BP (formerly known as British Petroleum) has a 100-million-barrel reservoir off the coast of Alaska. Rather, the reservoir sits on a BP-constructed island, and therefore it does not qualify as "offshore" at all. This seemingly large supply of oil will meet U.S. demand for less than a week, which presents a fine lesson in understanding large numbers. Meanwhile, long-time swing supplier Saudi Arabia is turning off the tap to ensure they have enough for themselves in the way of their own peak in 2005. So much for satiating our infinite desires with limitless oil from the Middle East. Even the International Energy Agency forecast demand in excess of world supply when they concluded we passed the world oil peak in 2006.

As world oil supply has fallen, the price has exceeded $80 per barrel three times in recent history. All three events were followed shortly thereafter by sovereign-debt crises in several countries. Considering the debt-related economic pain in Europe despite throwing money at the issue (i.e., papering over the economic mess), Keynesian economics makes no sense at all. The printing press hasn't been sufficient in the U.S., either, and it's the one-size-fits-all solution of the Obama/Bernanke team (and the preceding Bush/Greenspan team). This is the typical government approach: If it ain't broke, fix it until it is.

If you like Keynesianism, you'll love a couple ideas. First, we should establish a national holiday during which children are paid to throw rocks through windows, thus increasing expenditures on replacement windows. Then we should bomb the interstate highway system, which will require us to build new highways and new bombs. Just imagine the resulting economic "growth" (as perceived by followers of Keynes).

I'm not suggesting the debt-based approach hasn't been broken for a long time. But every attempt to "fix" the industrial economy represents a boondoggle atop a boondoggle, with every one destined for failure at a faster rate than the prior one. Helicopter Ben has created half the U.S. money in history within the last four years (2006-2010) even as the money supply continues to crash. On one hand, states want more federal stimulus (i.e., keep the presses running) as they head into an economic tsunami with no clue how to deal with it. On the other hand, pressure from taxpayers is building to stop or slow the printing presses, but it's already too late: We cannot possibly pay off the current U.S. debt, so -- from the perspective of presidents of the nation and the Federal Reserve -- there's no point in slowing the presses now, despite ludicrous, vacuous threats from various factions of the tea party. Meanwhile, the sheeple are growing frustrated as they wonder where the jobs went and why the industrial economy remains in the abattoir. Nobody in a position of influence has the guts to tell them about energy decline and its economic consequences; even if anybody with the ear of the people were talking about it, the hyper-indulgent sheeple wouldn't have the guts to listen, much less act on the knowledge.

The authority of the U.S. federal government has eroded to the vanishing point. No longer do the three branches of government possess significant authority. Their collective ability to right the listing ship of empire has been negated by forces large and small.

Whereas the president used to have considerable power, primarily through his position as commander-in-chief of the most lethal killing force in the history of the world, that power has slipped away. Oppression abroad is a primary tenet of American Empire, but our ability to oppress is diminishing rapidly, and the role of the military in a world heavily influenced by non-state actors is marginal at best. The president's ability to negotiate with other nations is sliding away as the world's largest economy is widely recognized as a banana republic. The U.S. dollar is the world's reserve currency, for now, but the president does not control the strength of a once-strong currency that is rapidly circling the drain. Finally, the president's ability to enforce obedience at home, another primary tenant of American Empire, has taken some serious body blows.

If the executive branch is wounded, the congressional branch is dead on arrival. Congress hasn't displayed even a passing interest in the lives of "ordinary" Americans for decades. Now that the latest version of gridlock has arrived on Capitol Hill, few people expect Congress to accomplish anything of significance. Because Congress has been intent upon transferring financial wealth from the masses to the wealthiest Americans, we should be cheering congressional impotence. The less the fools accomplish, the better.

Finally, there is the judicial branch. From the Supreme Court to the local courts, the judiciary has abandoned any appearance of fairness. They've become part and parcel of the ruling corporatocracy (i.e,. fascism). And without fairness as a guiding doctrine, the courts are worse than worthless. Although we incarcerate a greater proportion of our citizens than any country in the history of the world, our crime rate is stunningly high. Economic status and race are predictive of incarceration rates, making a mockery of the judicial branch. Although most people in this country fear the courts, few respect the courts or the judges. As with the other two branches of government, the masses have largely lost their confidence in the judicial branch.

When the citizens no longer respect the government, who is in charge? What prevents chaos from carrying the day? All the time, I mean, instead of periodically.

So far, I suspect chaos has been forestalled only by confidence in fiat currency. The Federal Reserve controls the printing presses. By buying U.S. Treasury bonds with Federal Reserve Notes (i.e., dollar bills), the Fed is able to flood the industrial economy with an increasingly worthless currency. As David Stockman, former director of the White House Office of Management and Budget, said in a November 2010 appearance on Bloomberg television, "the Fed is injecting high grade monetary heroin into the financial system of the world, and one of these days it is going to kill the patient." Each dollar entering the money supply represents a dollar of debt owed to the Federal Reserve by the U.S. government (i.e., taxpayers). For example, the $600 billion infusion (aka stimulus) cost everybody in the U.S. about $2,000. But you already owed more than you'll ever be able to pay, so what's a few more dollars, especially if they're worth less and less, and then nothing at all?

Ben Bernanke, the chairman of the Federal Reserve, is effectively king of the United States. His tenure as chair ends in 2014, and his appointment to the Federal Reserve board expires in 2020. In other words, we're stuck with King Ben until the ongoing economic collapses reaches completion.

In theory, the Fed is accountable to Congress. But in practice, nobody is Congress is particularly interested in exposing the Fed as a sham, so Congress whistles by the graveyard and looks the other way as the Fed conducts its business on behalf its owners. The Fed has been the de facto operator of the U.S. money system since it was established by the Federal Reserve Act of 1913.

Who are those owners? The Federal Reserve is privately owned, but ownership is a closely guarded secret. As a result, conspiracy theories are rampant. MSNBC has concluded the Fed owns itself, whereas many pundits raise the specter of ownership by the Bank of England or financial elites such as the Bilderberg group, the Rockefellers, or the Rothchilds. I doubt we'll ever know for certain, in large part because the owners do not want to be known and Congress is not interested in the truth. So we will continue to cede authority to King Ben -- and whom or whatever underlies his power -- as long as the empire stays afloat.

The Fed, working collaboratively with the executive branch, has created the biggest debt bubble in the history of the world. King Ben keeps pumping air into the bubble because he believes his mandate is to destroy downside risk in the stock markets, regardless of the damage to the dollar or the resulting cost of commodities (note the rising prices of oil, gold, and silver as Benny Bucks look for a place to land). There is little doubt $200 oil will kill a crippled industrial economy regardless how we get there, so Bernanke and the Fed are simply rushing us to the point of collapse with every bankster bailout. The latest dash of $600 billion cash is widely recognized as yet another bank bailout, but collateral damage includes increased prices of everything based on the U.S. dollar. There is no question this bubble will pop: the only questions are when and how loud. But this example of fraud is one many examples of a worldwide racket that is large and growing by the day.

It's about time to kick back with some popcorn and enjoy the show.

Continued deflation leads to collapse of the stock markets and therefore worthless fiat currency. The other economic option is hyperinflation, which leads even more quickly to worthless fiat currency. At the very least, the near future will bring increased volatility and a host of economic woes.

The water is boiling around us and, like frogs, we're failing to notice. Unlike frogs, we have the ability to see what's going on, and how it's killing us, but we prefer the culture of make believe over reality. So we pretend we're immersed in an imperial spa. Fever? What fever? I just need another drink. Apparently the cancer of industrial culture removes cognitive capacity before it kills the host.

Continuing to pretend won't help the dire situation on the housing front. As it turns out, housing and energy definitely are not too big to fail, with the attendant evidence mounting daily. Despite our best efforts to ignore reality, echoes of the Great Depression abound. As housing prices continue to decline, Americans lose the ability to use their homes as ATMs. As oil prices continue to increase, aftershocks continue to rumble through the system, with more quakes on the way.

And it's not just housing and oil. The collapse in commercial real estate is fully under way, banks are withholding information from the federal government because they dare not open their books in the light of day, another credit crunch lies right out the corner because nothing about the financial system has changed since the last crisis of confidence, and bond vigilantes are coming to America and therefore to the world's reserve currency.

GUY R. MCPHERSON

Plenty of people here in the empire think there are alternatives to oil, thus failing to distinguish derivatives from alternatives. These derivatives will never pay their way, of course, much less serve as anything resembling a comprehensive substitute to crude oil. And without abundant liquid fuels, we cannot grow the industrial economy.

Other folks believe hydropower will keep the lights on in their neighborhood, without working through the consequences of capitulation of the stock markets. Why would the engineers and technicians keep showing up to run the electrical plant if they aren't getting paid, either because all the banks fail or their employer's stock is worthless?

Too little, too late, Bill Gates and his ilk are urging us to spend billions on an energy revolution. But Gates and the gang are not spending their billions on it, probably because they know the fossil-fuel party is over.

As a result of running out of inexpensive oil on the way to passing the world oil peak in 2005, we witnessed an oil shock in 2008 that nearly brought the industrial economy screeching to a halt. Lord Peter Levene, who until 2010 was Chief Executive Officer of insurance giant Lloyds, warned of another price spike headed our way within a very few years, and I cannot imagine the industrial machine of planetary death surviving oil priced at the expected $200 per barrel.

But I'm an optimist. I think we can terminate the industrial economy before we move the assault from the Gulf on our southern border to the wholesale destruction of interior lands on our northern border even as it becomes increasingly clear the tar sands will not meet expectations. Events in the Gulf of Mexico illustrate an important point: As my detractors have been saying for years, we really are awash in a sea of oil. But you've got to be a psychopath to be happy about the events in the Gulf of Mexico (and virtually every other place on Earth, for that matter).

In support of my omnipresent optimism, historian Niall Ferguson has added his voice to the large and growing chorus predicting the collapse of U.S. empire in the near future. If we cease to kill the industrial economy, it will continue to kill the living planet and all

40

of us who depend upon it. Either way -- with imperial collapse or reduction of Earth to a lifeless pile of rubble -- we can stop worrying about power politics. As should be evident to any reader by now, I prefer a robustly living planet over a dying or dead one. As should be equally apparent to any sentient being, I don't have much company on this particular point.

Meanwhile, out in the dying Gulf of Mexico, BP has claimed success. Calls for a boycott are fading away and clueless Americans continue to display an inordinate capacity for cognitive dissonance as they continue to demand abundant cheap oil even while throwing the occasional tantrum at Exxon-Mobile, BP, and numerous other corporations that provide our drug of choice. You might go so far as to call this yet another example of American psychosis.

In short, the *Titanic* of ecological overshoot has crashed into the iceberg of limited oil, leading to a painfully slow descent of the industrial economy. The descent is painful because it allows us to keep the current game going, re-arranging the deck chairs as we head straight for a rapid decline in the human population in the wake of a devastated Earth.

There is a better way. We know what it is. It's time to give up our childish dreams and act like responsible adults. Is that too much to ask?

Belief, hope, and what I live for

I'm constantly amazed when people ask what I believe, what I hope for, what I live for, and so on. These seem, at least to me, to be personal inquiries, and what I believe is not relevant to what you believe. At least, I hope not. What I hope for should have nothing to do with what you hope for, except in the most general, generic sense. Ditto for what inspires each of us to keep on keeping on. And yet, the questions keep coming, even from people my own age and older. In this essay, I'll tackle these issues, one at a time.

What I believe

I try not to believe. Instead, I try to think. But it's sometimes difficult to separate the two, and it's often difficult to marshal enough evidence to allow thought to proceed unimpeded by belief. I suppose I'm skeptical, even about my skepticism. Usually, I think that's a good thing. And I recognize I'm quick to offend, especially when my words are unaccompanied by my smiling face and accommodating body language. Continue reading at your own risk.

I believe we spend too much time in the United States, and throughout the industrialized world, debating belief, and especially belief in spirits. And I believe we routinely confuse religion with faith or spirituality. I believe we shouldn't mislead children into believing there is a Santa Claus, an Easter bunny, a tooth fairy, a unicorn on the dark side of the moon, or a god. I think it's a sad commentary on the state of our cultural affairs that we finally get around to telling the truth about only the former five. Even sadder commentary is provided by the paucity of people who take time to think about what they believe, how they live, and what they hope and live for.

People who know me, even slightly, would describe me as neither spiritual nor religious. I do not believe in spirits, so I can understand the common conclusion about the former. I think organized religions are, to a great extent, absurd, violent, and immoral. When I think about the impacts of organized religion on society, I'm an anti-theist. But most of the time, I'm an indifferent rationalist, open to evidence but realizing faith is based on the absence of evidence. Or, as I tell the occasional student who asks, I believe in one fewer god than you. Unless you're Hindu, in which case I believe in 33 trillion fewer gods than you. I understand students asking these questions, by the way. They are still struggling to find their own ways, perhaps experiencing different world views for the first time.

I believe all life is loaded with religiosity. After all, religion is merely a set of beliefs and practices. Consider, for example, the set of beliefs and practices in my own uniquely quirky life: I'm a self-proclaimed rationalist and skeptic with a penchant for social criticism. In the latter role, I comfort the afflicted and afflict the comfortable with religious fervor. I *religiously* seek the truth (and I believe it should be spelled with a lowercase 't'). I *religiously* count steps when I'm walking, for reasons completely unclear to me. I *religiously* exceed the posted speed limit when I drive. And like Albert Einstein, I am a deeply religious unbeliever. And so on, ad nauseum. I suspect you get the point.

I believe Spinoza nailed the issue about religious spiritualism when he concluded that, if a triangle could think, it would imagine God to resemble a triangle. Upon learning this story, most people accuse the triangle of hubris.

I believe Nietzsche was correct about our lack of free will, and overwhelming evidence accumulated since his death supports this view. Nietzsche recognized that our ability to choose can overcome our lack of free will, but only with great intellectual effort (and, very often, intellectual suffering). Our absence of free will constrains, but does not eliminate, our freedom to choose. I believe education facilitates the process of choice over will -- that is, I believe education, when it works, is an intellectually painful process -- and I believe all education is, ultimately, autodidactic.

I agree with Jules Henry, in his classic 1963 book, *Culture Against Man*: "School is indeed a training for later life not because it teaches the 3 Rs (more or less), but because it instills the essential cultural nightmare fear of failure, envy of success, and absurdity." Public education in this country has become exactly the essential cultural nightmare it was designed to become by the likes of John Dewey and the United States Congress. It serves corporate Amerika by creating belief-filled drones incapable of deep thought. And, paradoxically, I believe John Dewey was right when he wrote: "Education is not preparation for life. Education is life itself."

In part because of the virtual absence of deep thought by mainstream Americans, I believe western civilization will suffer a profound and sudden collapse, thereby joining the two dozen major civilizations that failed before it (albeit at different rates, from different apexes and to different nadirs). I believe the collapse of civilization will be complete, in this country, within a few short years, and will be accompanied by human suffering that is unimaginable to most of us.

I believe this is a damned sad state of affairs.

I believe I will not live through the ongoing collapse. But I will fully engage the collapse, and act as if I will survive it. Acting "as if" is one rapid and appropriate way to ensure something positive will happen. Rosa Parks sat on the bus "as if" doing so were right. And, of course, it was.

Acting and living "as if" is a powerful approach to improving the human condition. It enables quick identification of the obstacles to improvement. It is the route to social change often espoused by contrarians and social critics (not to mention Buddhists). To live in opposition, as Christopher Hitchens points out in *Letters to a Young Contrarian*, "is not to be a nihilist. ... It is something you are, not something you do." Hitchens knows about our lack of free will.

Many people, including several friends, find it hard to believe I can go on, given what I believe (and especially what I don't believe). As if spirits, or faith in a life better than the one we get on Earth, make life worth living. As if one life is not enough, given its rarity and splendor. As if every day in ecological overshoot doesn't represent another day closer to our extinction, and the extinction of every other species on Earth. As if we need the promise of something else to carry on through our trivial existences on this celestial speck of dust at the edge of an insignificant galaxy. As if dying wasn't part of the deal from the beginning, for individuals, civilizations, and entire species.

What I live for

I have no problem finding things to live for, finding meanings in this most insignificant of lives, even though the life of a social critic has a significant cost: I have many acquaintances, but I've managed to offend most of my former friends. As an equal-opportunity offender, ever willing to speak truth to power, I'm largely an ascetic. To an increasing extent, I live as we all must die: alone.

One result of my abstemious existence, as we venture into the dark days ahead, is that I spend considerable time reflecting on my life goals and evaluating -- constantly re-evaluating -- what I live for. I have abandoned vigorous attempts to right the sinking ship of civilization, as well as half-hearted efforts to convince university administrators that my cause is just and therefore worthy. But my inability to adopt a completely hermetic life leaves me pathetically seeking solace from an indifferent universe, uninterested colleagues, and an increasingly distant family.

Obviously, it didn't start out this way.

As a carefree child in a tiny redneck logging town, I didn't have a clue. According to the many email messages I've been receiving about my lack of belief in a single god, I still don't. But that's another issue. I spent the 1960s and 1970s in youthful ignorance, chasing athletic fame and the girls who came with it. In college, hormonal lust had me blowing off a decent education while I majored in basketball and women's studies, even though Women's Studies departments weren't yet widely distributed, and there was not one on the campus of my misspent youth. I wasn't particularly good at either subject, and immature adolescence eventually gave way to a responsible life in avid pursuit of the "American Dream" of financial security.

To paraphrase author and social critic Daniel Quinn, the problem was not that I thought too highly of myself, or that I thought too little of myself, but that I thought constantly of myself.

As I was working hundred-hour weeks in graduate school and beyond, I was socking away the money and serving the cultural machine of western civilization. I was simultaneously reading and failing to heed the wise words of Edward Abbey: "All gold is fool's gold."

Somehow, though, despite my best attempts to hide from reality, I discovered that relationships are far more important than accomplishments. Stunningly, that occurred even before I earned tenure. Not surprisingly, I learned it from my students.

I tried to use a liberal approach during the second and final decade of my career as a professor. What does it mean to teach liberally? The obvious answer, which might even be correct, is found in the dictionary, where we find that liberal means "broad-minded" (among other things).

I agree with the dictionary but I don't think it goes nearly far enough. For me, liberal teaching means putting everything I know, and everything I am, at risk in the classroom. And not just in general, but specifically as well. That is, I put it all on the line during every meeting of every class. I've been wrong often enough to know it could happen again, and I'm willing to admit my errors in the pursuit of truth.

How courageous is this approach? Remember how it turned out for Socrates.

The essence of liberal teaching is taking risks every day. Rather than applying the conservative approach of deploying textbook knowledge -- the "I'm the teacher, and therefore I'm correct" approach -- a liberal admits his own humility, and celebrates our collective humility.

In my early years, I was a classroom conservative. Here's one minor example: I taught my dog to whistle. I taught, and I taught, and I taught. I used every trick I learned from graduate courses on college teaching. But my dog never learned to whistle. The problem with a conservative approach to teaching is the focus on the instructor and his wealth of knowledge, disseminated like so many pieces of valued wisdom to eager pupils (i.e., children, according to the etymology of the word "pupil").

A conservative approach to teaching ignores the reality and importance of diverse abilities and viewpoints, as well as our differential ability to perceive and understand various parts of the universe around us. By focusing on the authority figure, it ignores contributions from others. These others -- the ones paying for the opportunity -- have diverse life experiences that might, and often do, shed light on the topic under discussion. And perhaps even on life itself, and how it should be lived.

Not that we should broach such volatile subjects in our classrooms, of course. At least, that's what university administrators told me for decades.

Over the years, I came to understand and treat each group of people with whom I was fortunate to work as a corps of discovery. Our quest: a life of excellence for each of us.

Naturally, the quest was not welcomed by most students, at least not initially. In fact, I met considerable resistance each semester as I explained how a life of excellence can and should be pursued along the path of *Fire Management* or *Conservation Biology* or *Sustainable Living* (to list a few titular examples of courses I led recently). But by the end of the second week of each semester, resistance imposed by culture was overcome by the joy, humor, and richness of a liberal approach that valued contributions from every participant during every meeting.

An example might help. In February 2006, during the ninth meeting of a class titled *Wildland Vegetation Management*, the syllabus indicated the day's topic was conspicuous consumption. Already we're on tenuous ground from the perspective of the typical university administrator. During the first few minutes that day, somebody mentioned Siddartha Gautama (i.e., the Buddha) and his four noble truths. The link to conspicuous consumption should be apparent. Less apparent are the following topics, all of which we addressed within the first ten minutes of the class period, in this order:

No Child Left Behind (act)
Culverts under Speedway (a main surface street in Tucson)
The Princess Bride (film)
Charlton Heston (actor)
Sheryl Crow (singer)
John Dewey (pragmatist philosopher and educator)

47

Espresso Art (local coffee shop)

New Jersey Turnpike

Socrates

Pangaea

The conversation flowed naturally from one topic to another, and all topics were linked directly to the idea of conspicuous consumption. As traditionally taught, *Wildland Vegetation Management* is all about developing the means to continue our conspicuous consumption. As a group, we were questioning the validity of this historical approach within the context of popular culture and our own experiences.

As you might expect, I was not allowed to teach the course again (as is the department's head prerogative). Indeed, within a few months after the course was completed, and shortly after we hired a new department head, she banned me from teaching any classes in the department. She left the University of Arizona three years later, after making great strides in facilitating my own departure. She has taken her wrecking ball to her new job as a dean at another institution, but she departed too late to salvage anything worthwhile in my home department of two decades. From the vaunted heights of Dean-land at her new institution, she can quash a liberal approach at a much higher level than she was allowed at my own institution, at least for the short period during which the industrial economy limps along. Her neocon approach is exemplary as the ivory tower crumbles and becomes increasingly irrelevant to the lives of everybody involved in higher education. Indeed, I hardly fault her or contemporary institutions of higher education for pursuing the fool's gold of bricks, mortar, and economic growth, as demanded by culture.

Pursuing a liberal approach to teaching is dangerous. It requires courage, a thick skin, and recognition that the personal costs of pursuing liberalism in the classroom are far exceeded by the opportunity costs of failing to do so. Indeed, I would argue that the pursuit of a liberal approach to any of life's important activities is dangerous. That alone is sufficient justification to apply the approach at every turn, bearing in mind the words of Greek playwright Aeschylus: "Who refuses to listen, must be made to feel." (Quoting Aeschylus obviously contradicts my earlier comments about reason, thus confirming me as self-contradictory. That is, I am human.)

I left the ivory tower to work for The Nature Conservancy, only to find more of the same. I came back after only a year away and shortly thereafter taught Bill Calder's *Conservation Biology* course in the wake of this friend's death. It changed my life. It was the best course I'd ever taught because it was populated with students from more than 20 different majors, from creative writing to biology, none of whom was required to be there. During the autumn of 2001, we applied art and literature to the newly emerging enterprise of conservation biology in an attempt to bridge the two cultures of C.P. Snow (and Socrates before him, and E.O. Wilson after).

Needless to say, we failed.

Actually, we succeeded, in our own small way. Forty of us came together as a group, but society didn't come along. We had our bubble, but reality kept sneaking in and thwarting our efforts. Along the inspired journey, I learned something important, albeit small and personal: I had to serve, in my own small way, as a teacher and social critic and companion and friend and mentor. I had to bridge the two cultures, as if that's possible, and I had to show others how to do the same.

Along with this realization, I lost my anchor. Until I discovered myself, at the age of forty, I had believed science would save us. I had believed that rational thought was our savior. I had believed that, by abandoning fairy tales and magical thinking, we could find a secular way to enlightenment.

I failed to account for how badly scientists have lost their way. Science, as a process and a way of knowing, has unrivaled power. And you know what they say about power and corruption.

Actually, to be fair, science has not lost its way. Scientists have. They have been co-opted by objectivity, failing to recognize the impossibility of the task. They are unwilling to sacrifice their objectivity, which they do not and cannot have, in exchange for doing the right thing. Like everybody else, they are unwilling to make sacrifices to serve the common good. Indeed, many of them believe they are serving the common good, although they most often are confusing the common good with common culture.

Knowing culture will lead us astray, we nonetheless invite scorn when we seek the truth beneath the cultural current of the main stream. Culture does not have answers to meaningful questions. But skepticism for the sake of skepticism is no virtue, either.

Science is no longer my anchor. But teaching is, albeit in a different form than the years I professed in the classroom and asked questions in jails and other incarceration facilities. And I'm trying to live, for now, as if my life matters, as if it has meaning beyond the meanings I assign it. But I'm a lot more cynical and a lot less enthusiastic than I used to be about my tiny role in this grand play.

I still struggle every day to find meaning in a universe without meaning. Who shall I serve? For now, I can serve students of life and society at large by teaching and acting as if a single life can make a difference in a world gone awry. For now, I can demonstrate the value and importance of relationships, relative to accomplishments. For now, I can be kind to individuals while forcing institutions to do right, even if it means being unkind to individuals who represent institutions. For now, I can serve people by criticizing society.

And I can find meaning everywhere, in small observations and small acts. I can find meaning, and mystery, in cliff swallows and butterflies, the kindness of strangers, and a child's love.

But there's no role for a social critic when civilization collapses. What then?

It's too late to meet the three goals I had for myself as a teenager: Live fast, die young, and leave a pretty corpse. I'm too slow, too old, and too late, respectively. I'll have to continue seeking other reasons to live.

What I hope for

Dr. Day-Ruiner.

Dr. IHAN (short for I Have A Nightmare, wordplay on Dr. Martin Luther King's "Dream" speech).

Dr. Doomsday.

Prophet of Doom.

These are the names given to me by friends. They are among the nicest things people call me. You can imagine what others say.

Such is the cost of dealing in reality when we're ensconced in a world of make believe.

Fossil fuels are finite. Oil lubricates our economy. Without abundant supplies of inexpensive oil, our ideological monorail is headed for a cliff. That leaves our country with two choices: (1) commit to a steady-state economy or (2) go to war to get oil. We've been accelerating toward economic disaster since Jimmy Carter committed us to the latter choice in 1980: "Let our position be absolutely clear: An attempt by any outside force to gain control of the Persian Gulf region will be regarded as an assault on the vital interests of the United States of America, and such an assault will be repelled by any means necessary, including military force." At this juncture, several years beyond the world oil peak, disaster is the only option for the industrial economies of the country and world.

Of course I realize the consequences for living humans. Why do you think I rarely sleep? What do you think occupies my mind, every moment of every day and most nights? For starters, unimaginable suffering. Certain death for millions of humans. Probably billions. The Four Horsemen of the Apocalypse: War, Conquest, Famine, and Pestilence.

Do you really think I want this to happen? Do you really think I'm a fan of chaos, suffering, starvation, and brutal death? Do you really believe I have no empathy for fellow humans, seen and unseen? Do you really believe my goal is to generate fear, anxiety, and tears?

If so, you haven't been paying attention to what I say and write. The collapse of civilization dictates the loss of all the "money" in my retirement accounts. It indicates I'll be exposed to unimaginable suffering, and ultimately death -- likely sooner than later. It requires me to see -- and undoubtedly experience -- violence on a very personal level. And yet, the collapse of civilization is truly good news, if not for me personally then for all other cultures and species in the world. And also, of course, for future generations of humans on Earth.

As it turns out, chaos and a massive human die-off is better than what's happening now. The Four Horsemen have ridden into every corner of the globe, and have brought the apocalypse. Civilization has rained, and is raining, fire and brimstone onto the planet.

In short, civilization is the problem. It inflicts unimaginable suffering to nearly every species on the planet (excluding rats, cockroaches, and damned few others). It is the cause of unimaginable suffering for people in "uncivilized" cultures. As the last remaining superpower -- or, if you prefer, "hyperpower" -- we're strongly committed to destroying cultures and species as quickly as possible. We need finite, fossil materials to grow our economy, and we have the world's largest military. Therefore, we obtain the requisite materials by the usual and expected means.

As if those consequences of our greed are not enough, we're killing our own future, too. Unless we stop burning fossil fuels very, very soon, we're committing our children and grandchildren to a world that is uninhabitable to humans. And we're ensuring they'll be the last humans on this planet.

So, do I want to see it all come down? Personally, no. Like everybody else, I do not want to die young after suffering immensely (from the perspective of my students, it's too late for me to die young). But I'm wise enough to see beyond myself, and empathetic enough to give a damn about other cultures and species, and even future generations of our own species.

Call me silly, or any other name. But yes, I do want to see it all come down. And the faster the better, for the sake of everything on Earth that matters.

The sources of my hope can be found scattered throughout these essays. These sources are personal for me, as they must be for you. We must generate our own hope, one person at a time.

Sources of hope are distinct from what to hope for. Here's what I hope for: I hope we can power down with the tranquility of Buddhist monks. I hope we can get along with access to far fewer materials. I hope we can occupy small communities in harmony with the Earth and our neighbors. I hope humans occupy this most wondrous of planets at century's end, as well as in another thousand years. Most of all, though, I hope we can stop treating the world as a colony of American Empire. And with that hope comes the necessity to bring it all down.

As I cleared out the university office I inhabited for two wonderful decades, my thoughts turned to the nature of our future. I was asked to move out of my office the same month one of my articles graced the cover of the premier journal in my field, *Conservation Biology*. Although faculty members are fleeing my department like fleas from a drowning dog, the interim department head needs my office. It's the only faculty office in the building without a window, and I'm pretty sure nobody wants the space except the department head's graduate students. But that's none of my business.

And this collection of essays isn't about bitterness, anyway. It's about the decisions we make in light of an ambiguous future. One of the costs of making moral choices is breaking the strong emotional ties to a prior life. My own future, if I have one, is necessarily rooted in the past. So I'll start there, recognizing the inherent self-absorption of my approach.

For the better part of a decade, I was the model professor, if only from the standpoint of university administrators. I taught more courses than I was asked, completed more published research than nearly all my peers, and had an active record of service to various mainstream professional entities.

Then, realizing I had an obligation to the citizens paying me, I woke up and starting doing work of some import. As with most of the students in my classrooms, the citizens didn't appreciate me, at least not upon initial inspection. Learning is difficult, especially when unlearning is required along the way.

I maintained abundant activity of high quality in the three expected arenas of instruction, scholarship, and service, and I added one more delicacy to my overflowing plate: social criticism. I began to write for the general public, most frequently in the form of guest commentaries in various newspapers. My first opinion piece was an accident: When the university president refused to answer the letters I sent directly to him, I sent one of the letters to the local morning daily paper, thinking they might pursue it as a news story. They published it as a guest commentary. That very day, the president of the university responded to my earlier letters. And not kindly, either.

I was hooked. For the next decade, my opinion pieces focused on various aspects of faith-based junk science, including creationism, illiteracy, denial of global climate change, and denial of limits to growth. Since most of my colleagues were (and are) swimming in the main stream, my approach allowed me to simultaneously offend my colleagues as well as the public. In addition to writing for the taxpayers, I extended my service commitment to facilities of incarceration at the request of a new and soon-to-be dear friend.

In response to my newly discovered commitment to relevancy, and although I'd been the lowest-paid faculty member at my rank in the entire college for a decade, the administration soon ramped up the pressure. It wasn't long before I was viewed as a pariah on campus, and the dean of my college went so far as to libel me. Soon enough, I was banned from teaching in my home department and my scholarship and service were routinely denigrated.

But my students were learning to think, an aspiration reputedly revered but actually despised at all the large, research-oriented institutions with which I am familiar. Real education makes people dangerous. They might go so far as to question the obedience-at-home, oppression-abroad mentality requisite to propping up an empire. My Socratic approach was successful according to the only metric that mattered to me: real learning. The kind that sticks in your craw after you've fed at the trough of knowledge. The kind that gives a person the ability, courage, confidence, and desire to question the answers. The kind that changes lives, one life at a time.

Imagine the bittersweet nature of my departure. Recognizing the costs of imperialism, no longer could I tolerate living at the apex of empire, a large city. Recognizing the moral imperative of living outside the main stream, I left the easy, civilized life for a turn at self-reliance in a small community. Recognizing I was doing good work, and doing it well, was insufficient grounds to keep doing it.

I'm not sure I'd do it again, considering the contrary choice of my best friend. I certainly understand why, given a choice, many people would rather die than live outside the industrial economy. I understand, too, why most people who spend time at the mud hut depart with a renewed commitment to civilized living. After all, culture has convinced most people they have a personal investment in maintaining the industrial economy, rather than bringing it down. And it's clear to most of my visitors that this new life of mine is tough on the mind and even tougher on the body.

Judging from the overwhelmingly negative response to my departure from the hallowed halls, I chose the perfect age to change life pursuits. People older than my 49 years claim they don't have the energy, at their advanced age, to do what I've done. People younger than I claim they don't have the money to do what I've done (as if they could not join others, as I have done, by necessity *and* choice).

Although apparently I made the right choice at the right time, getting out of the industrial economy shortly before it reaches its overdue terminus -- and there is no unburning this bridge, even if I wanted to -- I have lost a majority of influence I might have had (as well as a majority of the ego-stoking limelight). Suddenly those three letters behind my name have lost their power. Because I am no longer active in the academy, I am not asked to deliver seminars at other institutions. I no longer teach classes through the honors college, which was willing to put up with my wacky ideas after my home department wasn't. I've moved too far away to serve populations in facilities of incarceration. And, from a strictly personal perspective, I miss the inmates and honors students with whom I was fortunate to work. I think about them and their wisdom every single day as I move endless tons of dirt, plant trees in the orchard, and make innumerable other preparations for thriving in the post-carbon era.

At the most specific level, few people face the choice I had. The proverbial brass ring of academia -- the tenured faculty position -- is a rare find. Once ensconced in the easy life of the ivory tower, particularly at the level of full professor -- or any other position for that matter, inside or outside academia -- few people would consider the implications of their lives for other humans and the entire living planet. At a more general level, I am hard-pressed to come up with any other person who would leave a high-pay, low-work job for any reason, much less morality. It occurs to me that forfeiting the easy life of tenured professor for the challenge of living outside the mainstream is the wackiest idea I've had yet. And I recently learned about a rumor circulating throughout the hallowed halls of academia: My insanity results from a rare disorder of the brain. I hope it's not lethal.

Clearing the final shelf of books as I cleaned my office, I turned to the last pages of my most comprehensive piece of social criticism, *Letters to a Young Academic*. The words seem a fitting finale to the chapter I've closed:

"I launch this paper boat with a final bit of advice about the life of the mind: Never take it for granted, for it could be snatched away tomorrow. The life of an academician is challenging, to be sure. It demands stamina of the mind and occasionally of the body. It requires personal sacrifice for the common good, a profession on full public display, and a predisposition to swim upstream against a strong cultural current. It is not for the faint of heart or the feeble of mind."

"But the rewards are supreme. You are allowed to live a life of leisure, in the historical sense: You choose the work you do. Through the lives of your students, you experience life and death and the wonderful emotional roller coaster of youth. As such, you can choose to remain forever young, if only vicariously. You have opportunities to serve as a mentor. And, if you are worthy and fortunate, somebody might endow you with that noblest of distinctions by calling you 'teacher.'"

THE ECONOMIC
APOCALYPSE

Saving the living planet from imperialism

Your medical doctor informs you: "You need to stop all industrial activities immediately, or you'll be dead in twenty years. And so will your five-year-old child. You might die between now and then anyway -- after all, nobody gets out alive -- but your death is guaranteed if you do not stop relying on fossil fuels for travel, heating and cooling, water from the tap, and food from the grocery store."

Naturally, you go straight from the clinic to the nearest store. You need liquor, and time to ponder whether the trade-off is worth it.

Late in 2007, the Intergovernmental Panel on Climate Change (IPCC) announced we were committed to warming the planet by about 1 C by the end of this century. Never mind that we were almost there when they reached this profound conclusion. Simply for elucidating the obvious, the IPCC was granted a share of the Nobel Peace Prize (climate-change crusader Al Gore received the other half).

A year later, late in 2008, the Hadley Centre for Meteorological Research provided an update, indicating that, in the absence of complete economic collapse, we're committed to a global average temperature increase of 2 C. Considering the associated feedbacks, such an increase in temperature almost certainly spells extinction of *Homo sapiens sapiens*, the "wise" ape.

In September 2009, the United Nations Environment Programme concluded we're committed to an average planetary temperature increase of 3.5 C by 2100. This leaves little doubt about human extinction by the end of the current century. Such a rapid increase in global average temperature almost certainly sets into motion a series of positive feedbacks that lead to runaway greenhouse, including decreased solar reflectance from light-colored surfaces due to melting of planetary ice, release of carbon previously locked in peat throughout the world's northern regions, and release of methane hydrates from deep beneath the world's seas.

In October 2009, Chris West of the University of Oxford's UK Climate Impacts Programme indicated we can kiss goodbye 2 C as a target: four is the new two, and it's coming by mid-century. Yet again, the latest scenarios do not include potential tipping points such as the release of carbon from northern permafrost or the melting of undersea methane hydrates.

In November 2009, the Global Carbon Project added to the increasingly miserable news by concluding that we're on a direct path to 6 C by 2100. The Copenhagen Diagnosis chimed in a couple weeks later with a scenario of 7 C by 2100. Between the release of reports by the Global Carbon Project and the Copenhagen Diagnosis, the United Nations concluded that, even during the miserable recession of 2008 when carbon emissions were expected to fall dramatically, atmospheric concentrations of carbon dioxide set new records, thereby matching worst-case scenarios of forecasting models only a few months old.

As if the ongoing series of assessments weren't gloomy enough, the International Energy Agency added to the agony in November 2010 when, in its *World Energy Outlook 2010*, it concluded the average global temperature on the planet will increase by 3.5 C in 2035. The United Nations followed up a month later with their latest and most dire assessment: 6.4 C increase by 2050. In other words, human extinction looms within a generation.

By now, the pattern is so clear even politicians and the media can recognize it: Each assessment is quickly eclipsed by another, fundamentally more dire set of scenarios. And every scenario is far too optimistic because each is based on conservative approaches to forecasting. Even an article in the mainstream scientific journal, *Climatic Change*, concluded in late November 2009 that only a complete economic collapse could stop the effects of runaway greenhouse from destroying the living planet. Although assessments do not include positive feedbacks, they also fail to include the notion of limited fossil fuels. If we terminate the world's industrial economy, we might stop runaway greenhouse.

The mainstream media periodically indicate what every sentient being fully understands: Carbon emitted into the atmosphere today will still be there in one thousand years, a 4 C increase in global average temperature spells the end of the line for our species, and we're headed there with astonishing speed. And yet, the media adhere with near unanimity to the misguided belief that a political solution lies within our reach.

Perhaps most sadly, every bit of dire news is met by the same political response, which has become expected to the point of being predictable. The Obama administration calls any attempt to reduce emissions "not grounded in political reality."

Is there any doubt we will try to kill every species on the planet, including our own, by the middle of this century? At this point, it is absolutely necessary, but perhaps not sufficient, to bring down the industrial economy. It's no longer merely the lives of your grandchildren we're talking about. Depending on your age, it's the lives of your children or you. If you're 70 or younger, it's you.

In 2002, as I edited a book about global climate change, I concluded we had set events in motion that would cause our own extinction, probably by 2030. I mourned for months, to the bewilderment of the three people who noticed. Less than two years later, I was elated to learn about a hail-Mary pass that just might allow our persistence for a few more generations: Peak oil and its economic consequences might bring the industrial economy to an overdue close, just in time.

If we abandon the industrial culture of death, we might persist until the children of today's world are old enough to die a "normal" death. But the odds are long and the time short. Barack Obama epitomizes the actions of every politician in the world by ensuring, with every political act, a miserable future and insufferable death for his wife and children.

Now I mourn because the solution is right in front of us, yet we run from it. We fail to recognize our salvation for what it is, believing it to be dystopia instead of utopia. What is the point in waiting for the last human on the planet to start the crusade? After all, completion of the ongoing collapse of American Empire has many advantages beyond survival of our species.

(American Empire is representative of, and acts as a leading indicator of, the world's industrial economy. And yes, I know all about use of the term "American" for the United States. Call me yet another imperialist.)

When American Empire completes its fall, we will not have the ability to sacrifice one big bank just to rescue an even larger corporate entity along with an ill-devised government program. Instead, we'll be focused on the only economic system too big to fail: Earth.

When American Empire completes its fall, it will take all the banks with it. So we won't be worrying about cleaning up "toxic assets." Instead, we'll concern ourselves with storing the harvest and saving seeds.

When American Empire completes its fall, political parties will be unable to carry out desperate, ugly, and dangerous attacks on American voters. Instead, we'll focus on helping our neighbors and building our communities, human and otherwise.

As American Empire is completing its fall, the American government might find itself at war with its own people. As long as we have *American Idol* on the television and high fructose corn syrup in the grocery stores, I doubt the people are willing to rebel. But if they are sufficiently motivated, perhaps this time the people will win.

When American Empire completes its fall, we will leave behind arcane philosophers and their irrelevant, unworldly philosophy. Instead, we will return to a philosophy as rooted in the Earth as we are. Think Socrates. Think Nietzsche. Think Aldo Leopold. *Think*.

When American Empire completes its fall, we will not have agents of the federal government planning to invade and divide countries, thus sacrificing the lives of "we the people" for a few bucks. For example, neoconservative leaders such as Feith, Wolfowitz, and Perle will be unable to plan how to divide a country on the radar of conquest (as they did with the Turkish ambassador regarding Iraq in the summer of 2001, four months before 9/11). Instead, we'll honor the lives of humans and other animals in the region we occupy.

When American Empire completes its fall, humans will be unable to kill the living planet. Instead, we'll revere the ecosystems that provide us with water, food, clothing, protection from the elements, and all the philosophy we'll ever need.

When American Empire completes its fall, the federal government will be unable to control what you eat, much less encourage you to eat toxic materials that make us fat, stupid, and lazy (such as high-fructose corn syrup). We will not rely on two percent of our population, bound to cheap fossil fuels and corporate indenture, to feed the rest of us. Instead, we will harvest what we sow and eat what we harvest, paying careful attention to what we feed our children.

When American Empire completes its fall, the federal government will not trot out lies about medical care (while in truly Orwellian fashion, calling it "health care"). Instead, we will learn to care for the planet that sustains us all, and we will accept death as we celebrate life.

When American Empire completes its fall, governments around the world will not encourage their citizens to produce more consumers (i.e., babies) in the name of economic growth (consider, for example, the recent suspension of China's one-child policy). Instead, we will cherish our (human) communities while relying on them for care, just as we will care for others. Instead of being slaves to the economy and its government, we will be partners with our neighbors and the landbase.

I used to think it took a child to raze a village, but now I know any effective politician can do it. When American Empire completes its fall, the federal government will be unable to bail out companies while ignoring the individuals who work for those companies (i.e., the federal government will be unable to practice the standard model of socialism for the rich, capitalism for the poor). The governmental arsonists who started and stoked the fire will be unable to show up in fire trucks claiming they can extinguish the blaze. And then they'll be unable to lie about it. When the empire completes its fall, neighbors will bail out each other, and expect the same in return.

When American Empire completes its fall, the myriad crises we have created will no longer outpace our ability to deal with them. The situation has become so dire, even mainstream scientists have noticed. And although these scientists admit nations and corporations cannot effectively deal with the messes we've generated, the solutions they propose all involve institutional reforms (i.e., government). When the empire completes its fall, communication between neighbors will account for all the reforms we need.

When American Empire completes its fall, globalization falls with it. Globalization has tricked us into ignoring matters important to our health, and to the health of other species, in the name of enriching a few wealthy (mostly) white men who serve corporations. We have abandoned work on extinction, child labor, working conditions, taxation, child labor, health, and pollution, while allowing more than a billion people to starve. We've done all this damage while allowing -- and even encouraging -- the few to loot the coffers of the many, even while the many are starving in numbers unimaginably large. When the empire completes its fall, localization comes back in style. We'll know all the non-human neighbors by name, and we will nurture them as they take care of us.

When American Empire completes its fall, we will not focus on the politically lost cause of global climate change at the expense of the thousands of other insults we are visiting on the planet. We won't need to focus on politically hopeless causes such as saving the planet and our non-human brethren. Instead, we will conduct the difficult and meaningful work associated with stewardship of the lands, waters, and communities that support us.

When American Empire completes its fall, the majority will not capitulate to the noisy minority in the echo chamber who claim that helping others is socialism, and therefore un-American. The notion that "all politics is local" will ring loudly as we all work toward governance that serves the people.

When American Empire completes its fall, we will not be forced to listen to the "patriotic" tune of the mainstream media as they continue to deny the roles of the governments of Israel and the United States in the events of 11 September 2001. And we won't be praying for more oil from other countries, much less stealing it. We'll stop believing natural gas will save western civilization, as if this or any other civilization is redeemable. When the empire completes its fall, we'll be concerned about legitimate wealth: food and water supplied by healthy landbases and the company of friends supplied by healthy communities.

When American Empire completes its fall, Congress will not spend your money propping up the world's most powerful military force (although by simultaneously losing multiple wars, the U.S. military is rapidly exposing its declining influence). We will not continue to torture people without charging them. We will not use the world's most lethal organization and weapons to continue killing citizens of Muslim countries in the name of our freedom. As a side effect, we'll need not hide the pictures and bury the stories when American children die in the process of killing Iraqis, Afghans, Libyans, Somalis, Yemenis, and doubtless others we'll add by the time this book is published. When the empire completes its fall, we will know the faces of those who threaten us and we will face reality regardless how tragic it is.

When American Empire completes its fall, we'll finally give up on the renewable-energy "savior" and, more importantly, we'll witness the end of the seemingly endless wars for energy. We'll live as part of the Earth, rather than apart from it.

When American Empire completes its fall, a few people will recall the warnings -- dating as far back as Marcus Aurelius, and probably further -- launched by a very few thoughtful voices and ignored by those in power. With respect to energy decline, they'll recall M. King Hubbert and the many people who followed him.

When American Empire completes its fall, people will once again wrest control of their individual and collective destinies and live in the world, thus causing superstition to fade.

If American Empire completes its fall soon enough, perhaps James Lovelock will be proven wrong: maybe, just maybe, we haven't reached a global-climate-change tipping point. One thing is clear: There are no politically viable solutions to global climate change. But when the empire completes its fall, we will ignore the gods of economic growth who demand we destroy the planet in their name.

Can we handle the truth?

The International Energy Agency (IEA) released *World Energy Outlook 2009* Tuesday, 10 November 2009. Even before the sham was shipped, it was exposed as a bucket of lies. Apparently U.S. presidential administrations think Americans can't handle the truth, so the administration applied pressure to keep the lid on the facts. If this country's paragon of transparency (i.e., world's leading liar) and master of hope (i.e., wishful thinking) actually trusted the American people, perhaps we could avert chaos.

If oil traders knew the truth about declining energy availability, the per-barrel price of oil would be $300 within a week. If stock traders knew the truth, we'd see capitulation of the markets shortly thereafter. If Americans knew the truth, they just might come to grips with reality, rally together, put their collective shoulders to the wheel, and start building a better world than the ominicidal culture of make believe to which we've all become accustomed.

But we'll never know, because the cabal of morally bankrupt bankers and politicians running this country -- and also the industrialized world -- will keep playing the shell game as long as they are allowed by the impotent media. Or, more likely, until the reality of oil priced in excess of $200 per barrel interferes with their imperial ambitions.

The consequences of the shell game extend well beyond economic disaster and the likely extinction of our species. In the short term, they include hijacking the world's marketplace, complete with child labor, hunger, and pollution (especially abroad), continued decline of intellectual "capital" in our universities, ratcheting up the war machine by attacking yet more countries (perhaps bringing a rapid demise to American Empire), further extending imperial overreach, continued shrinking of our credit-based economy, continued enrichment of the financially wealthy (including $100 billion for eight of Warren Buffett's companies), continued profiteering by the insurance industry, and continued land grabs in poor countries by wealthy countries. All with a U.S. military on the verge of complete collapse and despite widespread acknowledgment that American-style capitalism is not working.

To reiterate the choices facing us: (1) The economically dire truth and potential for chaos, now, or (2) Certain chaos and probable extinction, later. The moral certainty of the former choice is absolute. Perhaps that alone explains why we're choosing option number two.

Will reality intervene in time to save the living planet, including our own species? Stay tuned.

In the meantime, think about what you'd do. Let's play King For A Day. Would you trust industrial humans with the truth? Or would you commit us to chaos and probable extinction in the name of politics? In your response, think about wearing two hats: first your own, then, to make the game realistic, the hat of your favorite billionaire.

Abandoning a dream

I was among the final baby boomers born in the United States. Along with my entire generation, I owe the world an apology. My generation abandoned a worthy dream, and it will cost all of us, but nobody more than civilized members of industrial society.

My generation, which demographers say was born between 1946 and 1962, came together during Woodstock and the Summer of Love. We demanded environmental protection after we saw the Cuyahoga River catch fire and we demanded an end to the Vietnam War after more than ten thousand teenagers died in defense of capitalism. For us, environmental protection and peace were the same battle, and we won those battles, albeit temporarily. We started realizing our dream of living close to each other, and close to the land that sustains us all.

We lost our way during the late 1970s when the last decent president in this country called conservation, "the moral equivalent of war." But Jimmy Carter also laid claim to oil in the Middle East, declaring it U.S. property. We wanted to agree with him about both issues, as if they are not mutually exclusive. But, even more than we wanted environmental protection and peace, we wanted economic growth. So we threw away our dream, abandoned our principles, and snatched the brass ring. We threw Carter out of office after he asked us to slow down to 55 mph and put on our sweaters during the winter. We let a mediocre Hollywood actor convince us that it was, in his words, "morning in America." Like anybody who was paying attention during the gloomy days of the 1980s, I thought it was time for "mourning in America," and throughout the world.

The rest, as they say, is history. My generation consumed planetary materials -- calling them "resources" -- faster than any generation in the history of this planet. Instead of living in close-knit neighborhoods, we ramped up the suburban nightmare initiated immediately after World War II. Instead of living close to the land that sustains us, we trashed the world in a half-hearted quest for the short-term happiness that comes from accumulating material possessions, and then we traveled the world in a misguided spiritual quest, our lame attempt to "find ourselves." But all that consuming and traveling and trashing the planet is about to come to a rather abrupt stop because we've reached the point of "peak everything."

The extraction of finite materials tends to follow a bell-shaped curved, as M. King Hubbert described in 1956. The top of the curve is called "Hubbert's Peak," or "Peak Resource." Beyond the top of the curve, the human population continues to grow, thereby increasing demand, but the supply of the material declines. In this century, we have passed or will pass the peak of everything required to maintain civilization. For example, we passed the world oil peak in 2005. Peak silver is behind us, as is peak gold, peak copper, and peak uranium. Peak natural gas and peak coal lie on the horizon in full view.

If you haven't reached your 75th birthday, all you've ever known is economic growth. But that's rapidly changing. Passing the world oil peak led to oil priced at $147.27/bbl in July 2008, an event that nearly terminated western civilization. That event also brought Keynesian economics back from the 1980s, when Ronald Reagan used the Keynesian strategy -- and abundant, inexpensive oil -- to kick-start economic growth. This time's different, of course: There's no more cheap oil, and the Keynesian approach is a tiny band-aid on a spurting wound.

Kurt Vonnegut often described World Wars I and II as western civilization's first and second attempts, respectively, to commit suicide. He hinted at peak oil as our third attempt in his memoir, *Man Without a Country*, which was published shortly before his death in April 2007. I'm hoping peak oil and the consequent high price of crude oil will prove Vonnegut right in spelling the long-overdue death of western civilization and the associated liberation, for the living planet, from the oppression of industry. Call me quirky -- the government's term is terrorist -- but I'm a fan of life.

The financially wealthy burglar class runs the U.S. economy now, and they don't give a damn about my dreams, or yours. They're profiting, and profiteering, as the ship of industry goes the way of the *Titanic*. And, demonstrating as much wishful thinking as the architects of the plagued ship, they're calling this Greatest Depression "just a downturn."

For those of you who have never known anything except next year's I-pod, and have enjoyed the omnicidal industrial culture kick-started by Reagan's "morning in America," I have bad news for you: The ongoing collapse of the world's industrial economy will be complete within a few years. Soon enough, *American Idol* on the television, high-fructose corn syrup at the grocery store, and water coming out the taps will be distant memories.

On the other hand, for those of us who actually care about non-human species and non-industrial cultures, I have good news: The ongoing collapse of the world's industrial economy will be complete within a few years. Soon enough, *American Idol* on television, high-fructose corn syrup at the grocery store, and water coming out the taps will be distant memories. We will stop driving populations to extirpation and species to extinction. We will stop polluting the waters that slake our thirst. We will stop destroying the landbase that feeds us, clothes us, and shelters us. Many industrial humans will die younger than expected, but the survivors will once again be living the baby boomers' dream, close to their neighbors and close to the land that sustains them.

It appears the good times won't last long. Not only did the boomers destroy the living planet for other cultures and species, but we turned the dynamite on ourselves. Soon enough, the jig is up for *Homo sapiens*.

Human health: return of the four horsemen?

In the arena of human health, living in the post-industrial Stone Age will force us to deal with the biblical Four Horsemen of the Apocalypse. And I'm not thinking metaphorically.

During the time of Christ, in the Mediterranean region, the population of humans was viewed through the same lens as other populations. As such, human deaths often occurred in large numbers as a result of war, conquest, famine, and pestilence -- these are the Four Horsemen of the Apocalypse, as described in the gospel of John. The Four Horsemen of the New Testament are reminiscent of much of the Old Testament. Among the many exemplary passages in the Old Testament is this one from Deuteronomy: "The Lord shall smite thee with a consumption, and with a fever, and with an inflammation, and with an extreme burning."

Yikes. A quick review of the Old Testament suggests the Lord was partial to quite a bit of smiting. Strange and often fatal diseases were attributed to Divine Retribution. They still are, by some people. Not so long ago, President Ronald Reagan declared AIDS to be "God's revenge" on homosexuals. That was after he ripped the solar panels off the White House, but before he oversaw the military conquest of Grenada, a tiny island-country in the Caribbean most readers hadn't heard of, until then.

Until very recently, large-scale die-offs were viewed as "normal," in much the same way we view as "normal" our K-12 system of education, or weekly shopping trips to the big-box grocery store, or cellular telephones. The description and management of human populations during the days of the Greek Cynics was oriented along population lines, with relatively little societal regard for individuals. Contrast that perspective with our laser-like focus on individuals. Let's take a quick look at the Four Horsemen, one at a time. Famine's as good a place to start as any, considering that my limited understanding of human health tends toward eating. Or, rather, eating less, as we enter a time of poverty and starvation.

The years ahead will see a dramatic rise in deaths from starvation, as we become unable to transport vegetables from the Central Valley of California to any place in the country. The inability to retrieve high-fructose corn syrup in the form of cheese doodles and soda pop from the vending machine down the hall won't hurt us a bit, individually or collectively, but it's symptomatic of far greater problems. At the population level, starvation is called famine. And famine looms large, right here in the richest country in the history of humanity.

We'll also see pestilence -- what we call disease, when it happens one person at a time -- making a big comeback. Cheap oil allows us to sanitize our water, lethally cook harmful organisms, sterilize the surfaces on which we prepare and eat food, and manage many potentially catastrophic diseases. Contemporary American healthcare is completely dependent on ready supplies of cheap oil, for grid-based electrical power, backup generators, and thousands of pieces of equipment we all take for granted, from IVs and syringes to disposable gloves and plastic containers for tossing out contaminated needles and other sharp objects. When the trucks stop running, we won't even be able to deliver antibiotics, unless gigantic numbers of non-apocalyptic horsemen suddenly appear. I hope society will retain some understanding of germ theory, so our children are able to live at least half as long as their grandparents.

Famine and pestilence are two of the Four Horsemen; war and conquest are the other two. Already, resource wars have begun, and they are likely to ratchet up in the near future. The so-called bipartisan Iraqi study group concluded that Operation Iraqi Freedom was conducted in pursuit of black gold. In fact, just to make the acronym transparent, the invasion should have been called Operation Iraqi Liberty, as it apparently was during the early days of the conquest.

Regardless of the name of the invasion, it truly was "mission accomplished" for George W. Bush: We ensured ourselves a spot at the OPEC table, while also privatizing the oil fields of Iraq for American companies. Although the Oilman in the Oval Office correctly pointed out, in his 2006 State of the Union Address, "America is addicted to oil," his proposed solution is absurd. Rather than stressing conservation, as a conservative might do, his goal is to find more oil by any means necessary. Is that how to deal with an addiction? By finding more substance for the addict?

I fear Oil War III is just getting started.

And conquest is just another name for war, albeit without a fight from the vanquished. We've done that throughout our history, as have many other nations. I've no doubt we'll continue.

The Four Horsemen are lurking in the background, obscured by the never-ending, irrelevant chatter of the corporate media. The corporate media's weapons of mass distraction notwithstanding, soon enough the Four Horsemen will be riding tall enough for everyone to see. Population-scale rules from two millennia ago will re-assert themselves.

Socrates understood the importance of maintaining societal norms in the name of the law, even when justice failed at the level of the individual. And human-health practitioners back in Socrates' day undoubtedly understood that the good of the one, or of the few, sometimes must be sacrificed for the good of the many.

A lot has changed in the two thousand years that have transpired since Socrates drank from that fatal cup.

As an aside, I once asked a roomful of students, "What was Socrates' most famous quote?" I thought someone would answer with the one about the unexamined life being not worth living. Instead, somebody immediately yelled out, "I drank what?"

Many, and perhaps most, of the changes that have transpired during the last two millennia have occurred during the last century. We can trace many of those changes to American exceptionalism and our focus on the individual. In this country, we too infrequently take a population approach to human health. We decree every life worth saving, including the one-pound baby born 12 weeks premature, the 95-year-old with cancer in all the major organs, and everybody between. To a great extent, we have traded in a perspective on the population for an obsession with the individual.

Never mind human dignity. Our doctors are the best. They -- meaning we -- can save anybody. The costs, which are enormous, have been ignored in the name of vanity. These costs include economic, environmental, political, social, and moral.

Some countries have looked back to move forward. Ireland purportedly uses medical generalists in their communities to advance the public health. They preserve the good of the many at the occasional expense of the one, or of the few. Yet babies and old people die at the about the same annual rate in Ireland as in the United States. No, Ireland's public-health practitioners don't get to write articles about saving the lives of babies with no statistical chance of living. They don't get to bask in the reflected glory -- or maybe it's the hubris -- of their seven-figure salaries while their peers enviously wonder when they'll have a chance to break the new record. But perhaps, in focusing on communities and therefore letting go of some individual lives, Ireland has preserved something we've lost: something economic, environmental, political, social, or moral.

Linking the past with the present: resources, land use, and the collapse of civilizations

When man interferes with the Tao,
the sky becomes filthy,
the earth becomes depleted,
the equilibrium crumbles
creatures become extinct
(Lao Tzu, *Tao Te Ching*, ca. 550 BCE)

The human role in extinction of species and degradation of ecosystems is well documented. Since European settlement in North America, and especially after the beginning of the Industrial Revolution, we have witnessed a substantial decline in biological diversity of native species and profound changes in assemblages of the remaining species. We have ripped minerals from the Earth, often bringing down mountains in the process; we have harvested nearly all the old-growth timber on the continent, replacing thousand-year-old trees with neatly ordered plantations of small trees; we have hunted species to the point of extinction; we have driven livestock across every almost acre of the continent, baring hillsides and facilitating massive erosion; we have plowed large landscapes, transforming fertile soil into sterile, lifeless dirt; we have burned ecosystems and, perhaps more importantly, we have extinguished naturally occurring fires; we have paved thousands of acres to facilitate our movement and, in the process, have disrupted the movements of thousands of species; we have spewed pollution and dumped garbage, thereby dirtying our air, fouling our water, and contributing greatly to the warming of the planet. We have, to the maximum possible extent allowed by our intellect and never-ending desire, consumed the planet. In the wake of these endless insults to our only home, perhaps the greatest surprise is that so many native species have persisted, thus allowing our continued enjoyment and exploitation.

Although insults by *Homo sapiens* since the Industrial Revolution are well documented and widely acknowledged, abundant archaeological evidence indicates similar actions in the more distant past have led to the rise and fall of two dozen major civilizations. Humans clearly have impacted their environments since initially appearing on the evolutionary stage, and human impacts have grown profoundly since the development of agriculture and subsequent technologies (as reviewed by Charles Redman's 1999 text, *Human Impact on Ancient Environments* and, in more accessible prose, by Jared Diamond's 2005 book, *Collapse* [because I am not an anthropologist, I cite authorities in this chapter to a greater extent than usual]). Concomitantly, the environment has influenced the development of humans and their societies. The interaction between humans and their environments and the relative roles of culture and resources on human societies have received considerable attention from archaeological scholars. (The word "resources" is problematic because it implies materials are placed on this planet for the use of humans. We see finite substances and the living planet as materials to be exploited for our comfort. For efficiency and familiarity, I reluctantly use the word throughout this essay. I'll save the full rant for another essay while pointing out that my perspective is less imperial, and less Christian, than the traditional view.) The expansive literatures on resources, culture, and human-environment interactions indicate the important role of resources in constraining the development of several societies in the North American Southwest (as described particularly well by Timothy A. Kohler and colleagues).

Exploitation of ecosystems, even to the point of destroying fertility of soils, has constrained subsequent food production (as described most notably by J.A. Sandor and colleagues). Although I recognize the importance of these topics, I leave the continued study and discussion of culture, resources, and human-environment interactions in the distant past to scholars with more interest and expertise than me, and instead turn my attention to recent and ongoing assaults by humans on the living planet.

If we accept that humans played a pivotal role in loss of species and degradation of ecosystems -- and both patterns seem impossible to deny at this point -- we face a daunting moral question: How do we reverse these trends?

Maintenance of biological diversity is important to our own species because present and future generations of humans depend on a rich diversity of life to maintain survival of individuals and, ultimately, persistence of our species. In addition, as architects of the extinction crisis currently facing plant Earth, we have a responsibility to future *Homo sapiens* and to non-human species to retain the maximum possible biological diversity. We must embrace our capacity and capability to sustain and enhance the diversity and complexity of our landscapes. The substantial economic cost of maintaining high levels of biological diversity will pale in comparison to the costs of failing to do so, which potentially include the extinction of humans from Earth.

Reintroducing ecological processes with which species evolved, and eliminating processes detrimental to native species, underlie the ability to maintain and perhaps even restore species diversity. Specifically, the management of wildland ecosystems should be based on maintenance and restoration of ecological processes, rather than on structural components such as species composition or maintenance of habitat for high-profile rare species. In fact, a focus on the latter goals -- a fine-filter approach -- may clog the coarse filter necessary for landscape-scale management of many species and ecosystems.

Drivers of Change

The proximate drivers underlying changes in land cover during the first few decades after European contact were mineral extraction, agricultural expansion, timber removal, and introduction of nonnative species (most importantly, livestock). The quest for silver and gold drove the Conquistadors to dismember, rape, and murder native peoples throughout the New World. The effects of mining on natural ecosystems were no less dramatic. Even before fossil fuels were employed to ease the extraction of metals from the ground, waterways were diverted and steam-powered water cannons were used to blast soil from mountains. Every tree within several dozen miles of a mining operation was cut down or pulled from the ground to fuel steam-powered stamp mills. Trees that escaped the eye of mine operators rarely got away for long. The western expansion of the human population across North America drove great demand for construction lumber, railroad ties, paper products, and heat from the hearth. These changes and their consequences have been well documented in a wide variety of publications (see, for example, *People's History of the United States* by Howard Zinn, *One with Ninevah* by Paul Ehrlich and Anne Ehrlich, and *The Diversity of Life* by Edward O. Wilson).

Farmers and ranchers followed frontiersmen, trappers, and miners into western North America. Whereas frontiersmen left a relatively small ecological footprint and the operations of trappers and miners tended to be limited in spatial scale, agriculture dominated virtually every acre of the North American West. Row-crop agriculture covered areas with fertile soil that could be fed by irrigation systems, including nearly all rivers. The massive, arid expanses unable to sustain row crops supported the dominant form of agriculture: livestock. By the early twentieth century, cattle and sheep had trampled nearly every wildland acre in search of forage. Stockmen (and, rarely, stockwomen) led the charge to exterminate perceived predators and potential competitors for forage: wolves, bears, coyotes, eagles, and prairie dogs were among the species slaughtered in the pursuit of safe environs for livestock and those who grew them. Perhaps more important than direct mortality from shooting and trapping were pronounced changes in site conditions that resulted from the collective action of millions of mouths and hooves.

Livestock have had pronounced negative impacts throughout North America, and I think it is safe to call cattle the single most destructive force in the history of the American West. Livestock still loom large, and other biological invasions have transformed western landscapes. Some, like livestock, are politically "untouchable" despite adverse impacts on native species and ecosystems (e.g., "sport" fishes and various species of turf grasses critical to the golf-course industry).

Others are universally undesirable but seemingly intractable because of ecological, rather than political, reasons.

It is not surprising that we are largely unable to manage, much less eradicate, nonnative species. After all, there are more than 50,000 nonnative species in the United States alone, invading terrestrial ecosystems at the rate of 700,000 hectares each year at an annual cost of $120 billion; they threaten 400 species with extinction (these figures come from the excellent scholarship of David Pimentel and colleagues, most notably including their 2005 paper in the journal *Ecological Economics* titled, "Update on the environmental and economic costs associated with alien-invasive species in the United States"). To make matters even more challenging, every species on Earth is capable of invading other sites (as assured by biotic potential), and every site is subject to invasion by at least one, and potentially many, nonnative species. Because biological invasions depend exclusively on the "match" between characteristics of biological invaders and characteristics of sites, and because there are an infinite number of potential "matches" between species and sites, solutions to the problem of biological invasions are specific to species and sites.

Given the disinterest in environmental issues displayed by citizens and their elected representatives, I doubt we will seriously address the problem of biological invasions before we cause the extinction of own species. As such, this disinterest in environmental issues reflects ignorance or disdain for the living planet that sustains our own species. It represents, in other words, omnicide that will almost certainly prove fatal (kudos to Derrick Jensen for coining the perfect word to describe our murderous culture).

The transition to modernity brought infrastructure, notably cities and the ever-widening, increasingly well-maintained roads between them. Thus, within the last few decades, early drivers of change such as mining and agricultural expansion have been supplanted in importance by alteration of fire regimes, urbanization, and global climate change. Herein, I focus on the relatively simple impacts of each of these factors in isolation. As with historical drivers of change, interactions between these factors are complex, under-studied, and undoubtedly critically important.

A large and growing body of knowledge and empirical evidence indicates that fire was historically prevalent in North America, except in the driest deserts and the coldest tundra. It is clear that native species on the continent have evolved adaptations to periodic fires. Historical prevalence of fire ensures that even those species that seem most intolerant of fire have evolved in the presence of recurrent fires, as described in abundant ecological literature. Adaptations to fire are many and diverse, and include escape (e.g., distributions limited to rocky areas where fire rarely occurred), tolerance (e.g., thick bark), and rapid recruitment into post-fire environments (e.g., widely dispersed seeds and ability to establish in open environments).

Recognition that virtually all native species in North America evolved in concert with periodic fires leads to two general conclusions: (1) Native species have developed adaptations to fires that occur at a particular frequency, season, and extent; and (2) maintenance or reintroduction of the fire regimes with which these species evolved should assume high priority for those interested in maintaining high levels of biological diversity. A corollary to the first conclusion is that classification of native species along a gradient of adaptation to fire is simplistic and potentially misleading. Native species are "adapted" to recurrent fires, and classifying some as more tolerant than others suggests that fire is "good" for some species and "bad" for others. A more accurate view is that recurrent fires, at the appropriate frequency, season, and extent (i.e., components of the historical fire regime), are part and parcel of these ecosystems. A corollary of the second conclusion is that reintroduction of ecological processes should be a relatively efficient and comprehensive strategy for retaining native species in extant ecosystems. Indeed, the historical prevalence of fire in these ecosystems suggests that fire is a necessary component of any comprehensive strategy focused on retention of biological diversity. Because fire was -- and is -- a dominant process in these systems, restoration of fire regimes would seem to be an important first step toward maintenance of high levels of biological diversity.

Urbanization and the associated transportation infrastructure have divided formerly large, contiguous landscapes into fragmented remnants. Fires that formerly covered large areas are constrained by fragmentation, and animals that necessarily range over large areas, such as mountain lions, bison, and grizzly bears, have suffered expectedly. These changes have been particularly pronounced since World War II, largely as a result of government subsidies that have promoted growth of the human population and suburban development. These trends will be reversed within the next few years because the Oil Age is drawing to a close. Unfortunately, our near-term inability to burn fossil fuels on a large scale probably will come too late to save many of the planet's species from the effects of runaway greenhouse.

Ultimately, the story of western civilization is the story of fossil fuels. Profound changes in land use and land cover have been enabled by access to inexpensive oil and its derivatives (e.g., coal, uranium, ethanol, photovoltaic solar panels, wind turbines). Dramatic fluctuations in the price of oil within the next few years, coupled with steadily declining global supplies of this finite substance, likely will cause a complete collapse of the world's industrial economy, which might usher in a new era with respect to species assemblages and land cover. Given the dependence of humans on fossil fuels for power, water, and food (including production and delivery), it seems inevitable that many people will die younger than we've come to view as normal and the industrialized world's vaunted infrastructure will collapse, thereby giving other species a slim and dwindling chance to make a comeback. Although the pattern of dwindling access to resources and subsequent collapse of civilizations has been thoroughly described in the archaeological record, the ongoing collapse obviously exceeds previous others with respect to geographic scale, as well as the number of species and the number of humans impacted.

Peak Oil and the Collapse of Industrial Civilization

Oil discovery and extraction tend to follow bell-shaped curves, as described by M. King Hubbert more than 50 years ago. The easily reached, light oil is extracted first. Heavier oil, often characterized by high sulfur content, is found at greater depths on land and also offshore. This heavier oil requires more money and more energy to extract and to refine than light oil. Eventually, all fields and regions become unviable economically and energetically. When extracting a barrel of oil requires more energy than contained in the barrel of oil, extraction is pointless.

The top of the bell-shaped curve for oil extraction is called "Peak Oil" or "Hubbert's Peak." We passed Hubbert's Peak for world oil supply in 2005 and began easing down the other side, with an annual decline rate of one-half of one percent between 2005 and 2008 leading to a record-setting price of $147.27/barrel in July 2008. The International Energy Agency, which had never previously acknowledged the existence of a peak in oil availability, predicted an annual decline rate in crude oil in excess of nine percent after 2008 (so far, the annual decline rate has not come close to this figure). The current economic depression resulting from the high price of oil led to a collapse in demand for oil and numerous other finite commodities, hence leading to reduced prices and the rapid abandonment of energy-production projects. Many geologists and scientists predict a permanent economic depression will result from declining availability of oil and the associated dramatic swings in the price of oil. It seems clear the permanent depression is already here. The absence of a politically viable solution to energy decline explains, at least in part, the absence of a governmental response to the issue even though the United States government recognizes peak oil as a serious problem (along, no doubt, with many other governments of the world).

Without energy, societies collapse. In contemporary, industrialized societies, virtually all energy sources are derived from oil. Even "renewable" energy sources such as hydropower, wind turbines, and solar panels require an enormous amount of oil for construction, maintenance, and repair. Extraction and delivery of coal, natural gas, and uranium similarly are oil-intensive endeavors. Thus, the decline of inexpensive oil spells economic disaster for industrialized countries. Demand destruction caused by high energy prices is affecting the entire industrialized world.

Viewed from a broader perspective than energy, economic collapses result from an imbalance between demand and supply of one or more resources (as explained in considerable depth by Jared Diamond in *Collapse*). When supply of vital resources is outstripped by demand, governments often print currency, which leads to hyperinflation. In recent history, the price of oil and its refined products have been primary to rates of inflation and have played central roles in the maintenance of civilized societies. Addressing the issue of peak oil while also controlling emissions of carbon dioxide, and therefore reducing the prospect of "runaway greenhouse" on planet Earth, represents a daunting and potentially overwhelming challenge. Peak oil and the effects of runaway greenhouse are the greatest challenges humanity has ever faced. Tackling either challenge, without the loss of a huge number of human lives, will require tremendous courage, compassion, and creativity.

There is little question that the decades ahead will differ markedly from the recent past. From this point forward, *Homo sapiens* will lack the supply of inexpensive energy necessary to create and maintain a large, durable civilization. The fate of western civilization is in serious question, given our inability to sustain high levels of energy extraction. The population of humans in industrialized countries probably will fall precipitously if oil extraction turns sharply downward, as the International Energy Agency predicts. The benefit of a massive human die-off is the potential for other species, and even other cultures, to expand into the vacuum we leave in our wake.

This essay is extracted and modified from a book chapter celebrating 20 years of archaeological research in the North American Southwest (*Changing Histories, Landscapes, and Perspectives: The 20th Anniversary Southwest Symposium*). To improve accessibility for a general audience, I have removed references to the primary literature.

Resources and anthropocentrism

As indicated in the previous essay, the word "resources" is problematic because it implies materials are placed on this planet for the use of humans. We see finite substances and the living planet as materials to be exploited for our comfort. Examples of intense anthropocentrism are so numerous in the English language it seems unfair to pick on this one word from among many. And, as with most other cases, we don't even think about these examples, much less question them (cf. sustainability, civilization, economic growth). My only justifications for singling out "resources" are the preponderance with which the word appears in contemporary media, the uncritical acceptance of resources as divine gifts for *Homo sapiens*, and my essays on a few of the other obvious examples.

I'll start with definitions, straight from the *Merriam-Webster Dictionary*. Resource: 1 **a**: a source of supply or support: an available means -- usually used in plural **b**: a natural source of wealth or revenue -- often used in plural **c**: a natural feature or phenomenon that enhances the quality of human life **d**: computable wealth -- usually used in plural e: a source of information or expertise.

All these definitions imply an anthropogenic basis for resources, and c is particularly transparent on this point. Digging a little further, the etymology of "resource" brings us directly to lifelong bedfellows anthropocentrism and Christianity. "Resource" is derived from the Old French "resourdre" (literally, to rise again), which has its roots in the Latin "resurgere" (to rise from the dead; also see "resurrection").

From this etymology, it's a simple step back in time to Aristotle's "final cause" (which followed his material cause, efficient cause, and formal cause). Aristotle posited that, ultimately, events occurred to serve life, particularly the life of humans. This anthropocentric take on causality grew directly from the philosophy of Aristotle's teacher Plato, who focused his philosophy on separating humans from nature while popularizing the feel-good notion that humans have immortal souls. The idea that humans have souls, which was subsequently discredited by the (western) science that grew from humble Grecian roots, became the basis for Christianity, one of three Abrahamic religions that developed in the Mediterranean a few centuries after Plato learned from Socrates and then taught Aristotle.

Considering the history of western thought, it is no surprise we view every element on Earth as feedstock for industrialization. The only question for industrial humans is *when* we exploit Earth's bounty, not *if*. The logical progression, then, is to exploitation of humans to further feed the industrial machine.

Within the last few years, personnel departments at major institutions became departments of human resources. Thus, whereas these departments formerly dealt with persons, they now deal with resources. There's a reason you feel like a cog in a grand imperial scheme: Not only are you are viewed as a cog by the machine, and also by those who run the machine, but any non-cog-like behavior on your part leads to rejection of you and your actions. Seems you're either a tool of empire or you're a saboteur (i.e., terrorist).

It's time to invest in wooden shoes.

As if fifteen people are even willing to poke a stick in the eye of the corporations that run and ruin our lives. Why is that? Probably because we think we depend upon them, when in fact they depend upon us. And, to a certain extent -- to the extent we allow -- we do depend upon industrial culture for our lives. But only in the short term, and only as self-absorbed, comfortable individuals unwilling to make changes in our lives (even ones that are necessary to our own survival). Taking the longer, broader view, it is evident industrial culture is killing the living planet, and our own species. The cultural problem we face is not that we're fish out of water. Rather, it's that we're fish in a river. We don't even know there's an ocean, much less a landbase.

Aye, there's the rub. Evolution demands short-term thinking focused on individual survival. Most attempts to overcome our evolutionarily hardwired absorption with self are selected against. The Overman is dead, killed by a high-fat diet and unwillingness to exercise. Reflexively, we follow him into the grave.

On being a doomer

I admit I'm a doomer. But I don't think that's a bad thing. To be a doomer is to recognize the tragedy of the human experience and the limited persistence of organisms, civilizations, and species.

History provides some excellent company for those of us with doomer tendencies. Nietzsche and Schopenhauer are among my favorites. At the opposite end of the spectrum are those hopelessly optimistic writers and thinkers who don their rose-colored-glasses and conclude we can always find a way to advance civilization, and ignore its omnicidal aspects: Lester Brown, Paul Hawken, Amory Lovins, and many, many others in positions of power, including all national-level politicians.

Of course, power doesn't come to those who deal in reality (e.g., Nietzsche, Schopenhauer). Not only does no good deed go unpunished, but no bad act is unrewarded. Consider the following anecdote from renowned ecologist and Fellow of the American Association for the Advancement of Science Charles Hall, a professor at the State University of New York.

Hall has worked on ecological issues his entire career, and has been rewarded in the usual sense. He has received grant funds totaling millions of dollars and has published hundreds of papers. At the same time, he has spent his spare time working on energy issues, and has published more than 200 papers in this arena. But he has landed a total of $800 in grant funds to work on these issues, and he is perhaps the only person to be denied tenure from an Ivy League university the very week one of his papers landed on the cover of *Science* (the paper, which was far from radical, was titled, "Energy and the U.S. Economy: A Biophysical Perspective").

Obviously, Hall is not the only person who has been marginalized for his work on important issues. But his is a telling contemporary example of the type of infamy M. King Hubbert earned in his day, and a reminder how Cassandras (i.e., realists) are treated in any empire (at least as far back as Socrates).

Optimists, however foolish, earn external rewards. Realists are not so fortunate. On the other hand, realists get to deal in reality, and therefore face with honor the toughest judge: the mirror.

As I've written and said countless times, completion of the ongoing collapse offers the only legitimate opportunity for non-human species and non-industrial cultures to survive the onslaught of industrialization. The oppression at the hand of corporatism continues unabated, and has extended to all arenas of the human experience, including land-grabs by industrial powers at the expense the poor. If you're anthropocentric, it's worse than that. It's becoming increasingly clear that the industrial economy poses a threat not merely to national security, but also to the persistence of our species on the planet.

Which makes me wonder: When will even a small percentage of industrial humans join the doomer movement? Will the day come only after our species is reduced to a couple small groups of hungry individuals struggling to survive near the poles? Will we ever recognize the perils of human population growth? Or will we give up the planet, without so much as a muffled protest, as easily as we traded our republic for fascism (defined by Benito Mussolini as a merging of corporations and the state)?

More importantly, is that what we want? Is hell on Earth our goal for our hapless descendants?

The twin sides of our fossil-fuel addiction -- energy decline and global climate change -- are the most important topics we can address as a species. The national conversation ignores or marginalizes these critical topics. On the rare occasion they inadvertently come up, we act like a roomful of eight-year-olds with plates full of peas and mashed potatoes, pushing the main course around without actually ingesting it, wishing for the distraction of dessert.

Yes, I'm a doomer. And damned proud of the company I keep, too.

A typical reaction

Occasionally when people talk to me about my new life in and around the mud hut, their conclusions include one of the following statements: (1) You are selfishly wasting your talent as an excellent and inspiring teacher. You should be teaching at the university, saving students, instead of preparing for economic collapse. (2) Don't be silly. The United States cannot suffer economic collapse.

My responses go something like this: (1) At most, I made a minor difference for a few students during a two-decade career. I could keep doing that but, in the near future, that approach would kill me because it requires living in a major metropolitan area. I'm not willing to die for that particular cause. (The problem with being a martyr is that you have to die for the cause.) In addition, I can no longer teach the evils of empire while pursuing an imperialist life. (2) Have you failed to notice the economic world around us? We passed the proverbial end of the world as we know it when the suburban housing market collapsed. So we socialized Fannie Mae and Freddie Mac. Then we socialized the financial system and the automobile industry. Call it socialism for the rich, capitalism for the poor, to quote Paul Ehrlich and Anne Ehrlich in *One with Ninevah*. I'd guess we have a few years at most before there is no fuel at the filling stations, food at the grocery stores, or water coming out the municipal taps.

More often, the conversation goes something like the following. It typically includes a middle-aged, middle-class American (MAMCA) visiting with me, although my role often is subsumed by a student responding to his or her parents as they play the former role.

MAMCA: Nice place you have here. Thanks for the tour. Do you really think the economy could collapse?

Me: Of course. In fact, the collapse -- which, by the way, I prefer to call a Renaissance -- is fully under way. The U.S. industrial economy nearly came grinding to a halt several times (that I know about) during 2008 and 2009 in the wake of crude oil priced at nearly $150 per barrel. According to Dmitry Orlov, author of *Reinventing Collapse*, we're well into the latter of five stages of collapse (we passed financial collapse and we're in the midst of commercial, political, social, and cultural collapse although, unlike Orlov, I'd say social and cultural collapse have already happened in many locations, and we're poised on the brink of political collapse).

MAMCA: Well of course the Soviet Union collapsed. Everybody saw that coming. There is no way to sustain socialism, after all. But I don't see any way this country could suffer a collapse. How could that happen?

Me: First off, it's already happening, one household at a time. It could visit your household any number of ways. We passed the world oil peak several years ago, and demand seriously outstripped supply during the summer of 2008, when the price of crude oil topped $147/barrel. That led to the failure of the suburban housing market, the failure of several banks, and socialization of banks and General Motors. Unemployment is skyrocketing and the nation's "safety nets" are full of holes. Could you get caught in the unemployment wave? Probably not. Could you find yourself under water on your mortgage? Probably not. But many people, many households, have already collapsed under the weight of those two problems. Can you afford gasoline at $5 per gallon? Sure. But a lot of companies, large and small, cannot afford expensive fuel for a sustained period of time. When those businesses go under, they take real people down with them. At some point, all the banks collapse because the banking system only works when the industrial economy is growing. And the economy simply cannot grow when oil is too expensive because expensive oil eats up GDP. The typical approach with individuals, groups, or economies is the same: they grow or die.

MAMCA: Okay, but how do we get from expensive oil to economic collapse? How do we get to no water coming out the taps? I just don't see how that can happen. For starters, we'll develop alternative energy sources when needed.

Me: First off, bear in mind that an annual decline rate of only one-half of one percent led to $147 oil. The International Energy Agency, a group that previously never admitted oil would peak, projected a decline rate in excess of nine percent from 2008 forward. They've been wrong so far -- data indicate a far lower annual decline rate to date, and demand destruction in the form of the ongoing economic recession is staying ahead of the slow rate of decline of the extraction of crude oil. But if the recession shows signs of recovering, the price of oil will rise again. Oil priced at $150 per barrel consumes a large chunk of the world's GDP, leaving little slack in the system. Second, there are no "renewable energies" that scale to a few million people, much less a few billion. All energy sources are derivatives of oil, not alternatives: It takes a lot of oil to make a solar panel, or a wind turbine. And try putting those in your car or truck. The bumper stickers are right, after all: "Without trucks, America stops," at least with respect to growth of the industrial economy.

All that aside, would you continue to go to your job if you weren't getting paid, or if the paycheck kept bouncing? How about if money wasn't work anything?

MAMCA: I suppose not, at least not indefinitely.

Me: Would you continue to work if your employer has no financial value? That is, if the company is worth nothing on the stock exchange?

MAMCA: Of course not. That would mean they couldn't pay anybody. But I don't see how that leads to no fuel, no food, and no water out the taps.

Me: All fuel suppliers in this country are private. We have not nationalized our petroleum companies (yet). So if those companies have no value, do you suppose the drivers are going to keep delivering the fuel to the filling station? Ditto for Safeway.

MAMCA: Okay, I'll reluctantly agree that we could, eventually, have no fuel and no food. But no water out the taps?

Me: Who supplies your water?

MAMCA: I don't know.

Me: It's either a private company or, more likely, a municipality. The employees at the municipalities have to cash their checks, too. To do so, a bank has to issue the check and a bank has to cash it. Perhaps the more important question is, "Where does your water come from?"

MAMCA: The tap, of course.

Me: And if you believe water originates at the tap, you'll defend to the death the system that allows water to come out the tap. But of course water doesn't originate with the tap, it originates in the watershed. When people realize where the water actually comes from, perhaps they will defend to the death the system that supplies the water, meaning an ecosystem. But I doubt it.

MAMCA: What you're suggesting is that protecting the environment is more important than maintaining economic growth. But don't we need economic growth to have the money to protect the environment?

Me: I don't think we've ever made a serious attempt to protect the environment in this country. We occasionally take small steps to conserve specific areas after we ensure economic growth. But economic growth is the underlying root of environmental destruction. When we demand economic growth first, we postpone environmental protection until later. And it's getting very, very late.

MAMCA: What do you mean by that?

Me: According to recent projections from large climate-forecasting groups, we're very close to a tipping point, if we haven't passed one already. Global climate change is accelerating as a result of economic growth. If we don't halt or reverse global climate change, we're doomed to extinction at our own hand.

MAMCA: But we can't simply give up economic growth to save the planet, can we?

Me: No, apparently we're unwilling to take that step, sane as it seems. We'd rather reduce the planet to a lifeless pile of rubble than slow economic growth.

MAMCA: Surely we can have both economic growth and protection of the environment.

Me: I've never been shown how that's possible. Economic growth destroys habitats and species. Ultimately, it will destroy habitat for our own species, perhaps in as little as a single generation. We should welcome the ongoing Renaissance.

MAMCA: But no economic growth? You're committing my children to a future of poverty.

Me: No, you already did that. In fact, our entire generation of Boomers did that when we abandoned the goal of living close to the land and close to our neighbors for the sake of economic growth. When we were offered a choice between the good life and "morning in America," we chose Ronald Reagan and the notion that greed is good. As a result, we burned through the planetary endowment of fossil fuels at a record-setting clip, hence polluting our waters and skies while ensuring your children are addicted to fossil fuels, economic growth, and technology. But if they're like most 20-year-olds, they have no relationship with the living planet beyond the *Discover* channel and their Facebook friends.

MAMCA: An economic collapse sounds horrifying. People will die. Many of those people had nothing to do with this mess.

Me: As has always been the case.

MAMCA: What do you mean?

Me: The industrial economy is the basis of American Empire. Imperialism kills people every day, and most of them had nothing to do with this mess.

MAMCA: I was talking about Americans.

Me: So was I.

MAMCA: But many Americans will be caught up in the collapse. Most people in this country do not know how to live if there's no water coming out the taps.

Me: No, of course not. We've overshot our resources, and a sudden reduction in the human population is quite likely.

MAMCA: When faced with hard times, I'm certain Americans will change their behavior. The economy has always recovered before.

Me: On the back of cheap energy. But those days are behind us. We face an event unprecedented in the history of the planet. We can enjoy an economic collapse and the associated Renaissance or we can suffer ecological collapse. The Renaissance will cause human-population reduction, but not nearly to the extent of the latter. Some leadership on this issue would be nice, although it's clearly too late to save western civilization. Had we started on this project thirty years ago, we might be able to save some elements of civilization and avoid a large-scale die-off of civilized humans. But at this point, several years post-peak, I don't see how we can mitigate collapse at the scale of a few million people, much less three hundred million Americans or nearly seven billion planetary citizens. The famous Hirsch report concluded we'd have to start twenty years before peak to have a chance at saving civilization. And, even at that, we'd have to work at it. The federal government and the media haven't even acknowledged the issue yet.

MAMCA: Okay, so when does collapse hit?

Me: As I already indicated, it's already hit many people and many households. When does it hit you? That depends how wealthy you are. More importantly, it depends how willing you are to live in the world. I spent my life in the so-called ivory tower of academia. As you've seen, I've developed new skills to mitigate for a totally new set of circumstances in the years ahead. If I can do this, I'm pretty sure most people can, too.

MAMCA: I don't have enough money to do this on my own.

Me: Neither did I. My wife and I were fortunate to have like-minded friends who generously offered their property as a starting point. We still are fortunate. Very fortunate, as it turns out. But we can all do something to prepare, especially us middle-aged, middle-class baby boomers.

MAMCA: You seem to be taking all this in good humor. My daughter says you're a funny teacher, and I can see what she means.

Me: If you can't laugh at yourself, and you can't laugh at the apocalypse, you've got dark days ahead. On the other hand, if you *can* laugh at yourself, and you *can* laugh at the apocalypse, you'll never run out of material.

A review before the exam

Actually, this review is too late for the many people who have already endured economic collapse. As any of those folks can tell the rest of us, we do not want to receive the lesson after the exam.

This essay provides a concise summary of the dire nature of our predicaments with respect to fossil fuels. The primary consequences of our fossil-fuel addiction stem from two primary phenomena: peak oil and global climate change. The former spells the end of western civilization, which might come in time to prevent the extinction of our species at the hand of the latter.

Global climate change threatens our species with extinction by mid-century if we do not terminate the industrial economy soon. Increasingly dire forecasts from extremely conservative sources keep stacking up. Governments refuse to act because they know growth of the industrial economy depends (almost solely) on consumption of fossil fuels. Global climate change and energy decline are similar in this respect: neither is characterized by a politically viable solution.

There simply is no comprehensive substitute for crude oil. It is the overwhelming fuel of choice for transportation, and there is no way out of the crude trap at this late juncture in the industrial era. We passed the world oil peak in 2005, which led to near-collapse of the world's industrial economy several times between September 2008 and May 2010. And we're certainly not out of the economic woods yet.

Crude oil is the master material on which all other sources of energy depend. Without abundant supplies of inexpensive crude oil, we cannot produce uranium (which peaked in 1980), coal (which peaks within a decade), solar panels, wind turbines, wave power, ethanol, biodiesel, or hydroelectric power. Without abundant supplies of inexpensive crude oil, we cannot maintain the electric grid. Without abundant supplies of inexpensive crude oil, we cannot maintain the industrial economy for an extended period of time. Simply put, abundant supplies of inexpensive crude oil are fundamental to growth of the industrial economy and therefore to western civilization. Civilizations grow or die. Western civilization is done growing. After

94

all, you can't win, you can't break even, and you can't get out of the game.

Those three kernels are my favorite descriptors of the Three Laws of Thermodynamics. Respectively, the clauses mean (1) energy is conserved (First Law), (2) entropy never decreases, thus precluding perpetual motion machines (Second Law), and (3) it is impossible to cool a system to absolute zero (Third Law). The Second Law in particular puts insurmountable, irreversible constraints on everything we do. Without the Second Law, there would be no heat losses in energy systems, and electricity would be far too cheap to meter and commodify.

One way of looking at our current set of predicaments is that we've been on a binge, consuming energy considerably faster than it can be captured and stored by Earth's ecosystems. While fossil fuels once appeared limitless (and still do to deniers of peak oil), and though we're literally bathed in energy (in the form of sunlight), the disappearance of the fossil-fuel storehouse accumulated over millions of years isn't something that can be replaced with anything nearly as convenient as fossil fuels. Solar, wind, wave, geothermal, nuclear, and hydropower simply don't pack the same punch as fossil fuels, either singly or in combination. In short, we're falling off the net-energy cliff, and there's no lifeline to grab onto, no known technology to break the fall.

Long before the Industrial Era, work such as growing food, manufacturing goods, and distributing materials was accomplished via the limited power of human muscle (the monuments of the ancient world all being built with slave labor) and draught animals. Later, water wheels and windmills enabled us to convert force into mechanical power. The steam engine and combustion engine now allow us to tap the huge energy storehouse represented by fossil fuels and perform work we could not have done before, which translates into the sudden, exponential rise in human population and rapid destruction of the natural world. The differential between muscle power and simple mechanical power versus that harnessed by the application of fossil fuels can hardly be overstated. The trend from animal slaves (including humans) to fossil-fuel slaves seems like a one-way street, considering the paucity of draught animals and sanctioned slavery relative to the human population, but it isn't. Enslavement to fossil fuels ends when the now-abundant supply turns to scarcity, at which point radical austerity sets in.

Three attributes of fossil fuels are particularly noteworthy. First, fossil fuels -- especially crude oil -- have amazingly high energy density. If you've burned oak in a wood stove, you have witnessed the heating power of 6,000 Btu per pound. Depending on the type, coal contains 8,000-14,000 Btu per pound. The devil's excrement blows away wood and coal at nearly 20,000 Btu per pound. Once found, coal and oil are much more convenient to extract and deliver than wood, which explains in part why so many more railroad hopper cars are filled with coal than with firewood.

The second characteristic favoring consumption of fossil fuels is energy return on investment (EROI, sometimes expressed as EROEI for energy return on energy invested). Charles Hall is the primary authority on this subject, and his primer at The Oil Drum illustrates the importance of EROI while also showing how rapidly EROI has declined for U.S. oil. Specifically, average EROI of U.S. crude oil dropped from 100:1 in the 1930s to 30:1 in 1970 and down below 20:1 today while EROI for coal has varied from 40:1 to 80:1 during the same period. Meanwhile, firewood has an EROI of about 30:1, much higher than nuclear or solar photovoltaic (PV) and about the same as hydropower (we've nearly run out of rivers to dam and, at least in North America, we're tearing them down faster than we're building them).

The third big issue regarding fossil fuels is their potential energy. Coal and oil are just lying underground, containing dense sums of energy, begging us to gobble it up for our own immediate use, leaving nothing behind in the quintessential capitalist game of heedless maximization. There's no need to turn a turbine with the quaint use of wind or water to generate electricity. There's no need to bust apart atoms through exotic, risky, and expensive means that produce the nastiest of all wastes. Insatiable vampires, we jam our fang-like straws into the ground to extract easily combusted ancient sun-blood.

It's easy to understand why we committed to crude oil early in the industrial game. Its energy density, EROI, and convenience of combustion are irresistible, especially since we long ago ran out of whales to use for whale oil. It's small wonder, then, that we developed an entire civilization based on fossil fuels. The physics underlying the conversion of energy into heat, power, force, or work is a tangle of interrelated concepts not easily sorted out by nonscientists. However, whether various inputs and outputs are measured in watts, Btu, calories, joules, newtons, or volts, what's clear is that civilization is currently engorged, literally feasting on fossil fuels. But it's not anything close to a zero sum game, where resources stay constant and are only shifted around over time. Rather, the Second Law guarantees there is always a diminishing return.

Ultimately, all this points to a future in which we will be energy poor because we've used up the storehouse of cheap, convenient energy. In the not-so-distant future, the purportedly nonnegotiable American way of life, which is based on inexpensive and rapid movement of humans and materials via conversion of stored energy to mechanical power, will no longer be possible. Put in more immediate terms, there will soon be a time when old folks say with some nostalgia, "Oh yeah, I remember warm showers."

Not only is there no comprehensive substitute for crude oil, but partial substitutes simply do not scale. Solar panels on every roof? It's too late for that. Electric cars in every garage? Its too late for that. We simply do not have the cheap energy requisite to propping up an empire in precipitous decline. Energy efficiency and conservation will not save us, either, as demonstrated by the updated version of Jevons' paradox, the Khazzoom-Brookes postulate.

Unchecked, western civilization drives us to one of two outcomes, and perhaps both: (1) Destruction of the living planet on which we depend for our survival, and/or (2) Runaway greenhouse and therefore the near-term extinction of our species. Why would we want to sustain such a system? It is immoral and omnicidal. The industrial economy enslaves us, drives us insane, and kills us in myriad ways. We need a living planet. Everything else is less important than the living planet on which we depend for our very lives. We act as if non-industrial cultures do not matter. We act as if non-human species do not matter. But they do matter, on many levels, including the level of human survival on Earth. And, of course, there's the matter of ecological overshoot, which is where we're spending all our time since the first civilization began, and as described by William Catton in his thirty-year-old book, *Overshoot*. Every day in overshoot brings us more than 205,000 people to deal with later (every day on Earth, the number of human births exceeds the number of human births by more than 200,000 people). In this case, "deal with" means murder.

Shall we reduce Earth to a lifeless pile of rubble within a generation? Shall we heat the planet beyond human habitability within two generations? Shall we keep procreating as if there are no consequences for an already crowded planet? Pick your poison, but recognize it's poison. We're dead either way.

Don't slit those wrists just yet. This essay bears good news.

Western civilization has been in decline at least since 1979, when world *per-capita* oil supply peaked nearly coincident with the Carter Doctrine regarding oil in the Middle East. In my mind, and perhaps only there, these two events marked the apex of American Empire, which began about the time Thomas Jefferson -- arguably the most enlightened of the Founding Fathers -- said, with respect to Native Americans: "In war, they will kill some of us; we shall destroy all of them." It wasn't long after 1979 that the U.S. manufacturing base was shipped overseas and we began serious engagement with Wall Street-based casino culture as the basis for our industrial economy. By most measures of the industrial economy we've experienced a decline since 2000, so it's too late for a fast crash of the industrial economy. We're in the midst of the same slow train wreck we've been experiencing for more than a decade, but the train is teetering on the edge of a cliff. Meanwhile, all we want to discuss, at every level in this country, is the quality of service in the dining car.

When the price of crude oil exhibits a price spike, an economic recession soon follows. Every recession since 1972 has been preceded by a spike in the price of oil, and direr spikes translate to deeper economic recessions. Economic dominoes began to fall at a rapid and accelerating rate when the price of crude spiked to $147.27/bbl in July 2008. They haven't stopped falling, notwithstanding economic cheerleaders from government and corporations (as if the two are different at this point in American fascism). The reliance of our economy on derivatives trading cannot last much longer, considering the value of the derivatives -- like the U.S. debt -- greatly exceeds the value of all the currency in the world combined with all the gold mined in the history of the world.

Although it's all coming down, as it has been for quite a while, it's relatively clear imperial decline is accelerating. We're obviously headed for full-scale collapse of the industrial economy, as indicated by numerous statistics. Even *Fortune* and CNN agree economic collapse will be complete soon, though they don't express any understanding of how we arrived at this point or the hopelessness of extracting ourselves from the morass.

In short, we know what economic collapse looks like, because we're in the midst of it. What does completion of the collapse look? I strongly suspect the economic endgame is capitulation of the stock markets. Shortly after we hit Dow 4,000, within a few days or maybe a couple weeks, the industrial economy seizes up as the lubricant is overcome with sand in the crankcase. Why would anybody work when the company for which they work is literally worthless? Even if they show up for a few days to punch the time-clock, the bank will not issue a check, and the banks won't be open to cash it. It won't be long before publicly traded utility companies don't have enough employees to keep the lights on. It won't be long before gas (nee service) stations shutter the doors. It won't be long before the grocery stores are empty. It won't be long before the water stops flowing through the municipal taps.

There are those who question my credibility, particularly when I make predictions. We're in the midst of a war to save our humanity and the living planet, and some readers are worried about my credibility, as determined by the power of the main stream. My responses are two-fold: (1) I'm hardly sticking my neck out, unlike when I made my 2007 "new Dark Age" prediction by the end of 2012 (at which point the price of oil had yet to exceed $80/bbl, the industrial economy appeared headed for perennial nirvana, and everybody who read or heard me thought I was insane); of the fifty or so energy-literate scholars I read, nearly all indicate the new Dark Age starts before the end of 2012; (2) Get over it. This war has two sides, finally. This revolution needs to be powerful and fun, and we cannot afford to lose. We cannot even afford to worry about seeking credibility from those who are having us murder every remaining aspect of the living planet on which we depend for our survival.

Credibility? Respectability? It's time to stop playing by the rules of the destroyers. We need witnesses and warriors, and we need them now. It's time to terminate western civilization before it terminates us.

Lesson over. The exam comes shortly. And pop quizzes come up every day in this unfair system.

ACTION

Investing in durability

Industrial society is fully committed to tossing the planet in the waste bin. The throw-away products of the Industrial Age became particularly obvious after World War II, when the quaint idea of durable goods gave way to all the trappings of planned obsolescence. We invested heavily in items fabricated from non-renewable materials and specifically designed for one-time use, including now-ubiquitous diapers and grocery bags. And we made annual cosmetic alterations to every conceivable consumer product, from pens and kitchen knives to refrigerators and automobiles. Even consumer goods fabricated from renewable materials, such as wood, are routinely packaged in non-renewable materials designed for ease of discarding. The mass of transparent plastic wrap sold every day surely exceeds the combined biomass of all endangered species in the world.

At this point, there is no stopping the arc of history or the icons of industry. We're all hanging onto the roller-coaster ride of full-fledged economic collapse, which is fueled by the flawed notion of never-ending growth of the industrial economy. Unless you're planning to withdraw to an anarcho-primitivist society beyond the reach of the industrial world, there's little you can do, as an individual, to mitigate the damage to Earth or your wallet.

If you are planning to withdraw, please tell me where you're going, and send directions. If not, it's time to start thinking about how you and your family or tribe will muddle through the years ahead. One word comes to mind: durability.

If that wasn't the first word that came to your mind, I'm not surprised. Industrial culture has steered us, for the sake of economic growth, in the diametrically opposed direction for so long we usually fail to consider the obvious benefits of durability when making decisions about our own lives. It's time to change that pattern of thinking, time to start thinking about our own individual futures instead of the future of the empire.

First, let's consider what we actually need. Not what we want, which is the type of thinking that got us into this greed-induced mess. But what we actually need to survive as human animals. A group of students with whom I was fortunate to work recently laid the groundwork with a student- and southwestern-centric report (online at www.personalsurvivalskills.com). In this post, I focus on acquisition of a durable set of living arrangements for the post-carbon era.

Most accounts list at least three items requisite to human survival. We die within a few minutes without oxygen, within a few days without water, and within a few weeks without food. Each of these three varieties of death is allegedly painful and also uninteresting enough to merit much mention in the news (if you're going under, you might as well make a splash). In addition to these three items, many people add a fourth: some means of keeping body temperature at a relatively stable 37 degrees Celsius. The usual approaches involve a mixture of shelter and clothing, although we've been using fire to warm ourselves for millennia and fossil fuels to cool ourselves for a few generations.

In addition to these four items, I believe a fifth is imperative: human community. In the history of the planet, very few people have managed to live alone. Even fewer managed to maintain some semblance of sanity and happiness while doing so.

In this essay, I assume Earth's air will remain sufficiently toxin-free to support human life for the next several generations. This assumption likely is unmerited in light of global economic collapse and the consequent release of toxic material into the atmosphere as nuclear-power plants melt down without proper planning. But, in the spirit of my usual unwarranted optimism and our individual inability to mitigate for such a dire outcome, I will restrict my discussion of durable living arrangements to water, food, body temperature, and human community. I'll provide a few examples of the investments I've made, while advising the reader to think about durability for his or her own future.

The first and most important of my investments is not on my list of five items: information. After all, the more you know, the less [stuff] you need, so knowledge about surviving economic collapse is hugely advantageous. Considerable information is available at little or no cost via the local library and Internet search engines. The usual caveats apply: much of this information is worth exactly what you pay for it, and you'll need to provide the brainpower. I bought quite a few books, and borrowed many more from the library. Aric McBay provides an excellent primer with his brief book, *Peak Oil Survival*.

In the absence of fossil fuels, acquiring and delivering potable water is no minor task. Although age-old technology can be used to build aqueducts, I have a feeling we'll not return to that technology in time to save modern cities. As a result, I think contemporary cities are the worst possible places to be when the grid fails. Without access to water, it will be difficult to rally the increasingly irritated troops into constructing an aqueduct. And then there are the pressing issues of pressurizing the water-supply system, and getting rid of human waste in a safe manner. For the last few generations, we've avoided frequent, large-scale incidents of disease even while using potable water to distribute humanure throughout the entire civilized world. I doubt we can retain this indulgence much longer.

If cities are unviable, at least for large numbers of people, humans will be living in towns and rural areas, as we did for thousands of generations. For nearly all those thousands of generations, surface water was abundant and potable. Because of our historical and ongoing abuses to the planet, surface water has become scarce and undrinkable. As a result, we're left with rainwater, subsurface water, or a system of purification that does not rely on fossil fuels. Rainwater is relatively easy to harvest and use. I will not discuss the many types of filtration that can be used, but even a cursory investigation yields several alternatives, with a wide variety of costs and benefits. Subsurface water can be brought to the surface with wells dug by hand, particularly in regions with abundant rainfall where the water isn't far beneath the soil surface. Alternatively, individuals can harness fossil fuels to dig wells before the ongoing collapse is complete. Once the hole in the ground reaches the water level, a rope and bucket, hand-pump, windmill, or solar pump can be installed in the well to draw water to the surface. Life-giving water can be stored in cisterns, preferably far enough above the delivery point(s) to use gravity for pressure. Obviously, scaling up the acquisition and delivery of water to a few thousand people on the planet poses a serious problem. Scaling up to nearly seven billion human beings is almost certainly hopeless.

Water conservation is certain to come back into vogue. When we realize how precious water is, we will start using it more wisely. I suspect we'll become far more accustomed to the smell of the human body again, and I doubt we'll be using potable water as a vector for transmitting feces throughout the local area. A decent composting toilet is a great personal investment, especially if everybody in your neighborhood follows suit. At the mud hut, we have invested in rainwater-harvesting gutters and cisterns, a 3,000-gallon cistern for drinking water enclosed in a cinder-block wall, solar pump (with some backup parts), cast-iron hand pump, and composting toilets. The entire set of materials and labor, including the cost of drilling a new well, cost less than a new car. Given the primacy of water to every living thing, this investment is our most important one.

Food is similarly problematic for large numbers of people in the absence of fossil fuels for production and delivery. The industrial agricultural model relies heavily on inexpensive fossil fuels for manufacturing and applying fertilizer, pesticides, and water, and then again for harvesting, processing, and delivering food. In the United States, each calorie of food requires ten calories of fossil fuels, and the typical piece of produce travels 1,500 miles before reaching the grocery store. Obviously, this model of food production and delivery will not persist long into the future. And that's a good thing, since industrial agriculture -- the latest and hopefully last example of civilization -- is simultaneously killing us and the planet.

Assuming cities manage to secure water for their citizens, they will have profound difficulties acquiring and distributing food. Again, small towns and tribal collectives present significant advantages relative to modern cities. Intensive organic agriculture, which can be practiced locally with no fossil-fuel inputs, can produce food for four to six people on each cultivated acre, which is approximately 10 to 20 times the productivity of contemporary industrial agriculture. The resulting food is well-matched to the local environment and it need not undergo significant processing or travel great distances prior to consumption. As with water, however, scaling up the production and delivery of food to billions of human beings seems highly unlikely. As with water, I doubt the near future will see us wasting a large fraction of our food, as we do today.

Our investments include ample time with shovels at the mud hut. We also invest in heirloom seeds and seedlings, hardware cloth to protect trees and planting beds from pocket gophers, and compost and horse manure to mix with the native soil. We picked up free, hand-me-down composting bins for our organic material, and we installed a water-delivery system throughout the orchard and garden areas. Gutters collect water, and inexpensive cisterns store the water harvested from the roofs of the straw-bale house and the old mobile home; the stored water is applied to the garden beds. We built a chicken coop from straw bales and leftover corrugated roofing tin, and filled it with day-old chicks and ducklings that now provide about a dozen eggs each day. I've constructed a goat pen, as well as a predator-proof goat run. The goats provide milk, hence butter, yogurt, and cheese.

Food will be stored in root cellars, as well as in a deep-chest freezer powered by the off-grid solar system and a multitude of surprisingly expensive canning jars. Fruits and vegetables will be canned in the old-fashioned, wood-fired cook stove in the outdoor kitchen. Finally, I have rifles and a shotgun from my youthful days of hunting, and ample ammunition to harvest the occasional deer or javelina meandering onto the property.

Echoing the way we treat water from the taps and food at the grocery store, we take for granted clothing and structures that maintain the temperature of our bodies. Nearly all modern clothes contain petroleum, and the systems of producing fabrics, stitching them into clothing, and delivering the clothes to users all depend heavily on fossil fuels. As with clothes, we rarely question the fossil-fuel-intensive heating and cooling systems that maintain buildings at a comfortable temperature. Given the near-term demise of broad-scale access to fossil fuels, we will have to make other arrangements to maintain the temperature of our bodies.

As with water and food, cities are poorly suited for temperature regulation. Once the stores are picked clean of clothing, living in areas dense with human beings likely will pose significant dangers, including maintenance of body temperature at a constant 37 C. Individuals and small groups of individuals will rely on simple, archaic techniques such as wearing layers of clothing and hats for personal warmth. (You thought your civilized ancestors wore hats as a fashion statement?) Hand-me-downs will come back in fashion, and we will pay close attention to maintenance of our bedraggled pants and shirts. (I'm sure many people remember this one, although most of us haven't applied it directly for a while: A stitch in time saves nine.)

There is much information to consider in the arena of body temperature, and specific topics range from insulating buildings to layering socks. A healthy dose of common sense, a bit of thinking outside the proverbial box, and a couple of books by Cody Lundin are particularly valuable in this regard.

In a grand stroke of extravagance, we built a straw-bale house with superb insulation, passive solar heating (supplemented rarely with a small wood stove), and geothermal cooling. We pulled off this trick only by living frugally during a multi-decade, decently compensated career and then by cashing in our suburban home and everything else we owned, including life-insurance policies and retirement accounts. I bought a few pair of study work books, several pair of Carhartt™ pants (renowned for their durability), and plenty of sewing needles and strong thread.

I suspect community is the least regarded, yet most important, characteristic for the post-carbon era. All other preparations become moot if your neighbors take your water and food because they don't like you, or don't know you. Ready access to cheap fossil fuels has allowed us to ignore or disrespect people in close proximity while creating electronic "networks" of "friends." That problem's about to take care of itself.

A durable set of living arrangements necessarily includes substantive bonds between neighbors. If we are to thrive in the years ahead, we will need to share water, food, shelter, clothing, knowledge, stories, humor, and entertainment with the people in our community. I doubt we'll readily tolerate the kinds of behaviors exhibited daily by the typically hyper-indulgent twenty-something in contemporary America. People who do not make a positive contribution to durable communities face a never-ending struggle with thirst and hunger in the perennially too-hot or too-cold years ahead.

My investment in community is ongoing. I was fortunate to have the opportunity to develop a tenancy-in-common agreement with friends who have been valued members of their (and now my) rural community for several years. During the last few years, I have applied considerable elbow grease, my limited knowledge, and as much tact as I'm capable of mustering. I know these investments are necessary, and I hope they are sufficient, to get us through the challenging years ahead.

As we pass from the industrial age to the post-carbon era, the mantra of real-estate agents comes to mind. But the important factor isn't so much "location, location, location" as "community, community, community." The latter can be created in any location. Well, except for those locations the United States bombs into the Stone Age. It's tough to build community when the U.S. military is carpet-bombing the 'hood.

As with nearly every aspect of post-carbon survival, culture points us exactly the wrong direction when it comes to community. If you wanted to design neighborhoods specifically to eliminate interactions between neighbors, American-style suburbs would be the perfect place to start. If you wanted to further exacerbate the problem, you'd work hard to destroy public transportation in favor of automobiles (preferably at least one for each licensed driver in the house). Then you'd subsidize Big Oil so gasoline remained inordinately inexpensive relative to its actual cost, thereby further encouraging the use of community-destroying minimal-passenger automobiles. Finally, you'd create K-12 concentration camps and, if anybody tried to break out of culture's main stream, you'd incarcerate them on a more permanent basis.

In short, you'd transfer money from individual pockets to corporate kingpins while sucking the life out of communities. Take a look around: We're there. No country -- indeed, no culture -- in the history of the world has ever created a mess to match this one. We've created a system that requires cheap energy and, in the absence of cheap energy, defaults quickly to chaos.

How, then, do we build community? Start with the guidelines above, and then add at least the following:

Make yourself useful

Expect everybody to contribute

I'm sure I'm missing some important components. But when it comes to building community, any number can play, and everybody should play.

I am not trying to give the impression that our transition has been free from pain. We sold our beloved house in our beloved neighborhood, where we know and like all the neighbors. We had the spectacular Sonoran Desert in our back yard, and we were able to walk the dog through that desert off-leash twice a day (more, when she had her way).

It was the only house we'd ever owned, and we lived in it for 18 years. During those years, I'd seen two promotions, falling from untenured assistant professor to radical tenured full professor. And two sabbatical leaves, one to Berkeley, the other to a spectacular property owned by The Nature Conservancy adjacent to the mud hut. And a leave of absence to the Washington, D.C. metropolitan area, where I worked for The Nature Conservancy. And a few junkets to foreign lands. And 18 of our first 24 years of marriage, more than half our adult lives. And the death of our beloved first dog, and the deaths of a few family members. And the many simple joys of living in the Sonoran Desert, from curve-billed thrashers in the backyard palo verde tree to a handful of hummingbirds feeding on the nearby flowers, from frost on the creosote to sunsets and starry nights.

When we closed on the house, we cried half the night. And swore the other half.

Most people wouldn't even like the house, much less appreciate it. They certainly wouldn't live in it on purpose, if they had our combined incomes. It's strictly stick-and-stucco, emblematic of the poor architectural design for which the region is infamous. And it's a 1,000-square-foot house on a 4,000-square-foot lot on the edge of the city, too small for the gargantuan tastes of the average, over-indulged American. It's all one level, and incredibly low-maintenance, purposely planned for two people to grow old in. That was the plan: To grow old together, in the house we love, in the neighborhood we love, enjoying our lot in life and the opportunity for occasional travel to remote lands.

Along came Plan B.

If civilization doesn't fall apart within the next few years, I'm in real trouble with my partner. As if she hasn't had enough grief in her life lately, given the deaths of her mother, father, and uncle.

If civilization does fall apart within the next couple years, we're all in real trouble. And not just with my partner, either.

Seems I've backed myself into a lose-lose situation. You'd think I'd be accustomed to that by now, but I still hate it when it happens.

I suppose Bill Clinton was right: People like change in general, but not in particular. This is particular change, and I don't like it.

Living in two worlds is great in theory. But having to choose one world over the other is very, very difficult, especially when the choice runs counter to the status quo.

But now, late in the industrial era, is the time to push away from the shore, to let the winds of change catch the sails of our leaky boats. It's time to trust in ourselves, our new neighbors, and the Earth that sustains us all. Painful though it might be, it's time to abandon the ship of empire in exchange for a lifeboat.

After all, the time to dig a well is not when you're thirsty.

According to the Buddha, "life is suffering." And suffering is better than the alternative, at least for now. May we all find solace in our suffering in the months and years ahead. One way to mitigate that suffering is to invest in durability. Now is the perfect time to make

111

that personal investment, for myriad reasons. First and foremost, most sellers still think fiat currency is valuable.

I implore you to get started on your own durable living arrangements. American Empire provides bread, circuses, and all the toys we (think we) need, stolen from other countries and future generations. I can understand why people are reluctant to abandon the empire. In exchange for inhabiting a cubicle, you get to harvest the fruits of empire while avoiding any steps toward self reliance. You get to shower in the morning, kibitz at the water cooler with your friends, flirt with the hot thirty-something in the next cube, and dine on Thai take-out. What's not to like, especially if, like most Americans, you couldn't care less about the people we oppress to do your bidding or the costs to the living planet?

Immorality aside, there is a risk. The risk comes in two flavors. One flavor is the opportunity cost of abandoning the empire too soon. The other flavor is the bitterness that comes when you realize you waited too long to abandon the empire and you are suffering and then dying as a result. And surrounded by a bunch of ugly boxes we call suburbia, no less.

If you abandon the empire too early -- before the lights go out, before the shelves are bare in the grocery stores, before the water stops coming out the municipal taps -- you'll forgo some of those imperial fruits. On the other hand, you'll be ahead of the curve with respect to self reliance, you might ingratiate yourself into your community, and you'll learn how to live on little. We're all headed that way, with the ongoing economic collapse likely to reach your house within a matter of a few years and perhaps much earlier.

The second risk is the larger one, and also the more tempting one. It is based on your proclivity for dining on the fruits of empire a bit too long. I hate to get biblical, considering my beliefs, but if you hang on to the easy life in the city too long, the wages of sin is (sic) death. To take a more secular approach drawn from popular culture, try this line from *No Country for Old Men*: "This country's hard on people, you can't stop what's coming, it ain't all waiting on you. That's vanity."

So far, this country's been very easy on people (especially Caucasians), one of the consequences of ready access to inexpensive oil. But that's changing, and it's about to change much faster. You can either get in front of the changes or you can let them roll over you. Think steamroller, and you're a duck in a leg-hold trap.

Would you trade your human community for an online community? Some people with whom I speak are so reluctant to give up their sixteen daily hours on Facebook they'll gladly sacrifice human interaction for the joy of electrons. They will be hammering away at the keyboard long after their "friends" stop answering, long after the batteries run dry in the laptop, long after the grid has failed. Waiting, waiting, waiting until there's nothing left to wait for.

Would you trade virtual reality for reality? Some people with whom I speak are so reluctant to give up their television shows they'll willingly sacrifice human interaction for the feel-good dumbassery of television characters. They will be wondering what happened to their "friends" on television long after the television blinks out for the final time. Then they'll wait for a studly hero to save them. He'll be otherwise occupied.

Would you give up living because you fear the future? Some people with whom I speak are so unwilling to give up the notion of marauding hordes they'll turn away from personal preparations for a decent future because they fear their preparations will be insufficient. Such a decision thus becomes a self-fulfilling prophecy: The collective unwillingness to prepare. We make our own futures, albeit constrained by reality. But some people with whom I speak are unwilling to make changes in light of a changing world, thereby ensuring change will happen to them instead of with them.

Would you trade your life for medical care? Some people with whom I speak are so reluctant to give up their employment "benefits" they will work until the industrial age ends. And then work a while longer, hoping insurance will cover their trip to the clinic for a flu shot. All the clinics will be closed.

Would you trade your life for a night on the town? For me, it would have to me a helluva night. Some people with whom I speak are so reluctant to give up eclectic and inexpensive (sic) restaurants and nightclubs they'll keep their date with Destiny's Child, thus sealing their own destiny.

Would you trade your life for a few bucks? How about for a lot of bucks? Some people with whom I speak are so reluctant to give up their puts and contracts in the markets -- after all, there's serious bling to be made off their expansive knowledge of peak oil and the financial markets -- they will be trying to make money off their next trade long after the lights go out, thus precluding electronic trading in the belly of Wall Street's beast.

Would you trade your life for the industrial economy? Some people with whom I speak are so reluctant to give up inexpensive (sic) groceries they are waiting until the industrial economy finishes its collapse. Then they'll move. Or, more likely, they won't.

Would you risk your life on the Technomessiah? Some people with whom I speak are so reluctant to give up their easy lives in the city they'll bank on the ability of technology to bail us out of our dire economic mess. They fail to recognize that inexpensive oil is the Technomessiah. She died a few years ago, but she's walking around, zombie-like, to save on funeral expenses. Burying a messiah isn't cheap, you know.

Would you risk your life on the government? Any government? Some people with whom I speak are so reluctant to give up a high standard of living at low (sic) cost they'll count on the ability of the government to keep the toys and jobs coming, courtesy of American Empire and its militaristic reach.

Would you trade your sense of humanity -- your ability to become a human animal in the real world -- for meaningless chit-chat at the water cooler? Some people with whom I speak are so reluctant to give up interpersonal interactions in the workplace they'll gladly forgo the wonder of the human experience in a human community. They willingly, gladly, purposely hang onto a murderous way of living in exchange for the good life (sic).

Would you risk the lives of your progeny, and all future humans, for the comfort of inexpensive (sic) fossil fuels? Some people with whom I speak are so reluctant to give up happy motoring and central air conditioning they'll gladly ignore the cultures and species we destroy on our imperial path. By their actions, if not by their words, they demand a personal IV of cheap oil, just as this country mainlines crude.

What will it take before you notice the warning shots? If you think the empire cannot fall within a few short years, you're reading a different set of tea leaves than the dozens of petroleum geologists, social critics, thought leaders, writers, historians, and economists to whom I've been paying attention.

What will it take before you notice the moral imperative? I'm not thinking about the morality of attending church services or donating to the community food bank; rather, I'm thinking about the real costs of everyday choices based on cheap living within the mainstream culture of the industrial economy.

What will it take before you begin preparations for a world of your own making? The real world awaits, beyond the edge of empire. And if you don't think the United States represents an empire, then I don't think you understand the meaning of the word.

Rome is burning. Why are you fiddling?

Building community

Several years ago, anticipating the day when gasoline would not longer be available at the corner gas station, when food would no longer be available at the grocery store, when water would no longer come through the municipal taps, when the U.S. industrial economy comes screeching to its overdue end, I gathered a few friends and acquaintances to start talking about making other arrangements. The process of "selecting" people for the conversation was spontaneous, arbitrary, and inclusive. I'm not sure how some of the people stumbled upon the information, but about thirty of us found our way to an initial meeting at my house.

We met every week or so, but the list of people dwindled quickly. This was expected. Everybody was plenty busy with their "regular" lives, denial runs deep in the empire, and a little of me goes a long way (I attended every meeting). We shopped for land, and even came very close to closing on a rural property, with a passive-solar house not far from Tucson. The group declined in size and level of commitment as we came ever closer to pulling the proverbial trigger. Eventually, after slightly more than a year, attrition was nearly complete.

Importantly, my wife and dog were still "in," at least as much as ever. But we were back to square one, this time on our own.

Shortly thereafter, we attended the memorial service of a friend. Among the guests were two people, along with their four-year-old son, who were in the early group of thirty. They opted out of the process early because they love their current human community and the 2.7 acres on which they live. Imagine our surprise when, at the close of the memorial service, they offered us their west acre.

We declined. But the offer began a conversation that concluded, a couple months later, with a tenancy-in-common agreement for the property. We began building the straw-bale house and other infrastructure as time and money allowed. A year later, we'd made a small start toward post-carbon living arrangements. And we'd learned a lot about growing plants, building infrastructure, and nurturing each other. It was a wild ride, filled with moments of deep disappointment, simple pleasure, and wondrous, unexpected elation.

116

Never mind the mutt of a puppy. Did I mention I have a child in my life? Who'da thunk it?

If you're thinking about relocating, there is much to consider. Will your new location have advantages in any or all the important arenas of water, food, shelter, and -- perhaps most importantly -- human community? At this point, you'll be among the last people into your new area. You'll be the "other" all humans seek when times get tough. I don't think cities are survivable in the years ahead, but being a stranger in a rural area poses its own set of problems.

Consider a minor example from my own misspent youth, in the midst of this country's cultural revolution. Five years after my family moved to a tiny town just the other side of nowhere, we were still the new people in town. I was a typically ignorant 10-year-old walking to elementary school in the morning when a 13-year-old neighborhood bully pointed a gun at my head out his bedroom window. I didn't run and, in return, he didn't pull the trigger. When my family moved seven years later, we were still the new people in town. Rurality has its advantages, but don't expect to become part of the community overnight on the strength of your good looks. At least, it didn't work for me.

This short essay falls far short of expressing the heartache associated with the collapse of our initial effort, the one with thirty people trying to build a community. An enormous investment in time and effort ended in failure because the entire enterprise was far more challenging than any of us imagined it would be. The increasing urgency of this topic demands frank conversation, but the human ego is stunningly fragile. As a general strategy, I would not recommend starting the conversation about relocation with a group larger than half-a-dozen people, primarily because you'll need to create and maintain an emotionally, psychologically, and physically functional group of people, on short notice, to do things you cannot imagine doing. The future is funny that way: We don't even know what needs to be done.

If you think familial relations are tough, multiply the difficulty by a billion or so, and then factor in the notion of spending the rest of your life in close proximity to these people.

The obstacles to creating a decent human community and moving to self-sufficiency are simply too numerous to list here. If you're interested, I recommend a few books and websites to get you started (a comprehensive list is nearly infinite, but these resources will lead to many others). Books include Aric McBay's *Peak Oil Survival*, Dmitry Orlov's *Reinventing Collapse*, and Matthew Stein's *When Technology Fails*. But there are many, many more, covering relevant issues from many different angles. Websites are abundant, at least while we still have them, and include an online report on survival in the post-carbon era prepared by a few of my students as an independent-study project (www.personalsurvivalskills.com).

Ultimately, I suspect the longevity of your life depends on making excellent decisions in the absence of reliable information, along with a large dose of luck. With that cheery thought, good luck to us all.

The service trap

I recently reviewed the memoir of a friend and former student who, at the tender age of 24, is a poet, teacher, and retired cage fighter. His yet-to-be-published memoir will be his third book. *Caged* focuses on the traps in which he's found himself, and the way out of those traps. Late one summer night, when I should have been sleeping, I recognized a trap he had failed to identify. It applies equally to me. It's the service trap.

This example, though, is from Cameron Conaway, former poet in residence at the University of Arizona's renowned poetry center. He shows up as scheduled at a nearby Indian reservation, prepared to teach creative writing to elementary-school kids. The teacher forgot he was coming, so she sent him away. Most reasonable people would have pocketed the money and gone back home. Not Cameron. He wandered the campus, poking his head into various classrooms, asking how he could help. After a few attempts, the special-education teacher let him teach geometry.

This is a minor example in an exemplary life, a life filled with service to others. What combination of DNA and personal history allowed -- nay, required -- Cameron to pursue a life of service? For starters, Cameron is plagued, like to the rest of us, by the absence of free will (which is not to be confused with absence of choice). But how did he get there? How did any of us?

The odds against any one of us being on this most wondrous of planets exceed the odds of being a single atom plucked from the entire universe. Combine our inherent uniqueness with our one-of-a-kind personal history, and I daresay it'd be impossible to ascertain how any of us ends up doing what we're doing.

It is clear that some of us are committed to lives of service, and others are not. I'm sure social scientists have identified myriad patterns to justify our quirky lives, without actually explaining them, much less identifying mechanisms underlying them. And that's just as well, given the magnitude of the task. I'd rather we spend our considerable cognitive surplus on other issues. Consider, for example, how much time we spend tweeting on Twitter. And then trying to determine if twittering counts at literature. Never mind who's drinking which brand of beer in the White House. We're so absorbed with television and the Internet and who's screwing whom in the world of celebrities, we can't bother to focus on the inordinate suffering we're causing to humans and other animals. Sixth great extinction, including our own species? Whatev. Solving those problems will simply have to wait until after I get a tattoo proclaiming my independence from mainstream culture.

Better days lie ahead, in part because service will be all the rage. If you're not serving your community, your community won't be serving you. Cheap fossil fuels allowed us to trade in a life of service for a service economy. When we re-localize, we will not be able to rely on Facebook "friends" for moral support, much less for heavy lifting. It's time to start carrying our own weight, and a little extra for our community.

One way to make a contribution is to spread the good news about collapse of the industrial economy. Indulge me a personal example, if you will. During the autumn of 2008 I delivered a presentation, by invitation, at a conference about wildfire in San Diego, California. I spoke at length about the impacts of fire-suppression activities on natural communities. Anybody who's spent a little time on the fire line and paid attention knows that the adverse consequences of quelling a fire often exceed the adverse consequences of the fire itself. I started with a little Greek philosophy and a quote from the *Tao Te Ching* (see the introduction of the essay titled, "**Linking the past with the present: resources, land use, and the collapse of civilizations**"). Then I talked about the impacts of fire-suppression activities on natural communities for nearly 20 minutes, along the way pointing out the obvious: When the world's industrial economy collapses, as it surely will, we'll no longer need to worry about the impacts of fire-suppression activities on wild nature. Peak oil made an appearance on four of the 48 slides, and I spent about five minutes on the topic.

The first question came from the back of the room: "Are you for real?"

My first thought was to enter the realm of postmodern philosophy, thus allowing me to return to the philosophical beginnings of my presentation while probing the nature of our existence, individual and collective. But I don't think that's what he meant, so I played along. I then spent considerable time explaining the ongoing collapse in clear language that almost nobody was willing to understand.

Denial runs deep in the empire. It was as if they'd never heard of a recession before, much less a depression. Or a Depression.

Back in Tucson a few hours after engaging a room of denial, a second reminder of how we can commit to lives of service appeared in the cover story the local counter-culture rag. The compelling story, told sufficiently well to evoke tears as I read it, described *Poetry Inside/Out*, a program in which writing intersects with jail, forgiveness, and humanity's future. It reminded me that we can do many things to help others and ourselves as the world comes down around us.

Frequently, I am asked, "Why bother?" After all, if we're about to be rocked by world-changing catastrophe, shouldn't we focus on helping ourselves, instead of others? To which I can only respond, "Why not bother?" If we cannot help others navigate turbulent waters, what is the point to life, and the point to living? Whereas I admit we must save ourselves to help others, worrying only about personal survival is not interesting to me.

I know, I know. Some of my readers think the world is not coming down around us. But, for the girls in the detention facility and the guys in jail, the roof has already caved in. Fortunately, several of us chose our date and place of birth with considerable care, so we've been immune from lives filled with hate and hatred, impoverishment and poverty, disinterest and disharmony. And the inordinate amount of wisdom that results from a life on the "wrong" side of wealth, hence justice. Trust me: Our time is coming. For many of us, it's already here.

My recommendation, for those who care about humans and our share humanity: Get active. Witness some hard times, and help people who are experiencing them. You might be surprised what you'll learn from people you hear described as "stupid" and "poor." You might learn about real riches, instead of the illusory ones. And I guarantee you'll learn about wisdom, if you're wise enough to pay attention.

For those readers who are willing to take a more proactive approach, there are thousands of steps we can take to shorten the industrial economy. We need to take many actions, large and small, to bring it all down. I speak, write, and pull survey stakes. I burn as much oil as I can afford, and I turn on the lights in public buildings. I ask inconvenient questions, speak truth to power, and point out absurdities even when it hurts (me, that is ... it always hurts those about whom I'm speaking).

So, then. What are you going to do?

Balance is for Buddhists

Balance is a central tenet of Buddhism, foundational to the four noble truths and the eight-fold way. Balance is a superb notion and I strongly support, for individuals at least, balance, moderation, and many other principles of Buddhism. Indeed, had Buddhism found roots in this country a couple hundred years ago, we probably would have avoided, or at least delayed, the series of catastrophes we now face. But with fewer than one percent of the American population dedicated to Buddhism, it's a little late for balance and moderation to work their magic at the scale of this country, much less planet Earth (as if even one percent of Americans give a damn about planet Earth).

I'd like to subvert in advance the notion that we can give peace a chance. Industrial humans possess "freedoms" only because our governments employ a massive, non-stop war machine to keep us "free." And don't give me that "love it or leave it" crap. I stopped loving this country a long time ago, so I tried to make it better. A quick look around reveals how well that worked for all of us. At this point, the only escape from American Empire involves feeding on beetle juice in the caves of Tara Bora, and I'm having too much fun seeing the industrial economy give way to nature's patience to jump off the imperial ship at this late juncture. Put simply, peace (i.e., the absence of war) doesn't stand a chance. As Ran Prieur points out in the superb documentary film *What a Way to Go: Life at the End of Empire* (I'm paraphrasing): From the perspective of any particular location, the dominant paradigm of oppression and hierarchy always wins. If a peaceful people occupy an area, and a violent tribe comes along to conquer them, there are three possible outcomes: (1) the peaceful people leave, thus committing the area to the dominant paradigm of oppression and hierarchy, (2) the peaceful people fight back, thus committing the area to the dominant paradigm of oppression and hierarchy, or (3) the peaceful people choose to become slaves to the violent tribe, thus committing the area to the dominant paradigm of oppression and hierarchy. Give peace a chance? Not on this planet. And that's just our relationship with other humans, about whom we actually claim to care.

Back to the point, then: It's too late for half measures. Perhaps it always was. Half measures will not save the industrial economy, as U.S. politicians are discovering with each gargantuan new bailout. The bailouts, perceived as necessary to keep the industrial economy lurching along, barely manage to keep the trucks running and the water flowing from the taps, and only by passing to future generations the bill that will never be paid. Half measures certainly won't save the living planet, despite the pleas, petitions, and calls to arms issued by mainstream conservationists for the last several decades. These conservationists are making a decent living in the industrial economy, fiddling while the planet burns. But they are patently ineffective at saving anything except their way of life. And they're the good guys.

If the middle way is no way at all, what's left? I propose getting rid of the omnicidal monster called western civilization, and sooner rather than later. We've already had enough globalization, enough just-in-time delivery of meaningless baubles, enough sight-seeing and food-tasting and basking in the "good life" at the expense of every life form on the globe. We really do not need every American high-school student making the obligatory trip to Rome and Florence to see another culture (sic).

Instead of extracting an easy life from fossil fuels and human slaves, while taking our life-support system down into the bowels of hell with us, let's try living as our predecessors did on this land. Never mind abandoning our beloved cars: In North and South America, we'll need to give up the wheel.

I'm willing to give up every single piece of industrial civilization to see it all come down. An electromagnetic pulse (an "e-bomb") would be a fine start. Yesterday would be the perfect time, but tomorrow will suffice. Indeed, I'll gladly die if that's one result of civilization's fall. Personally, I suspect both will happen within the next few years. But I look upon this exciting, once-in-a-lifetime event as a chance to substantively experience the world around me, perhaps for the first time. It's also a personal challenge and a superb opportunity for personal growth, all without purchasing a round-trip ticket to Rome.

By way of a thought experiment, what elements of industrial culture would you choose to save? I'm not suggesting you have a choice, mind you. Rather, I think the ongoing collapse of industrial culture will remove most of the choices for all of us. And, as infamous war criminal Henry Kissinger fondly pointed out, "the absence of alternatives clears the mind marvelously." But let's beat Henry to the post-industrial party, shall we? Let's imagine what we can get along without, even before it's gone.

I'll get us started by assuming we want to save electricity (i.e., continue killing every part of the living planet so we can comfortably read our Harlequin Romance novels). The following extremely generous back-of-the-envelope calculation illustrates part of the costs needed to build solar panels to run the U.S. electrical grid:

The total energy requirement to produce a PV panel is about 1,000 kWh per square meter, and there's about 1,700 kWh in each barrel of oil. My math skills aren't what they used to be, but this ain't rocket surgery.

In the U.S. alone, we use about 4 trillion kWh for electricity annually. I'll generously assume 30 percent efficiency of solar panels. The solar constant is 1.4 kW per square meter, so we need slightly more than 2 billion square meters of solar panels to satisfy current U.S. electrical demand (i.e., the 4 trillion kWh): 1.4 kW per square meter x 12 hr/day sunlight, every day x 0.3 {the efficiency conversion} x 365 days/yr = 1,840 kWh/yr, and 4 trillion Kwh divided by 1,840 kWh/yr = 2,174,385,736 square meters.

It takes about 1,000 kWh of energy to manufacture a single square meter of PV panel. So we need a tad more than 2 trillion kWh of energy to manufacture the solar panels needed to keep the grid going.

Because each barrel of oil contains about 1,700 kWh of energy, we need about 1.3 billion barrels of oil to manufacture the solar panels needed to keep us supplied with electrical power in this country. We use a little less than 20 million barrels of oil each day in this country, so we could forgo oil for about two months to stockpile the oil we "need" to keep the grid running (except, of course, that we haven't accounted for shipping, installation, storage of electricity, or maintenance of the panels or the grid). Draining the strategic petroleum reserves (SPR), which currently contain 727 million barrels of crude oil, would provide a little more than half the 1.3 billion barrels needed to make the panels.

Skipping oil for a month or two, much less draining the SPR, would destroy the industrial economy almost overnight because traders on the world's stock markets would hit the panic button. Needless to say, I'm completely in favor of the idea.

If you foolishly prefer the nuclear option for electricity, consider these points: (1) Nuclear is more expensive than fossil fuels, so I have a hard time believing Americans will willingly pursue this route; (2) We have no idea how to deal with the waste, despite decades of talking around (vs. about) this issue; (3) Nuclear power plants do not become carbon neutral for at least two decades because cement production (and use) is so carbon-intensive (and after 20 years or so, we start shutting the plants down because of safety concerns); (4) Energy too cheap to meter, if it ever comes, will reduce the living planet to a lifeless pile of rubble within a generation; (5) I seriously doubt the industrial economy has time to build many, if any, nuclear power plants; (6) The economic impact will be minimal, regardless -- the industrial economy runs on oil, which is required to maintain the electrical grid (and nuclear power plants); and (7) we're past peak for nuclear sources.

I'm sure I'm missing several salient points and I haven't addressed many, many other issues. What elements of industrial culture will we lose when the industrial economy completes its collapse? Which of these elements do you value more than life itself (the lives of others, of course, not Americans)?

Think of the benefits associated with all of us giving up every aspect of western civilization. Goldman Sachs unable to manipulate the market, as they've done since the Great Depression. More importantly, the Milky Way shimmering in the night sky. The absence of suffering (Schopenhauer's version of happiness) as we realize we are no longer witnessing the only mass extinction our species has ever seen (and the only mass extinction caused by a single species). No more bad news about our destruction of the living planet. No more good news about collapse of the world's industrial economy. No news at all, except the kind delivered by a smiling neighbor on foot.

But that's my dream. What's yours?

A ten-step plan for furthering civilization

I don't believe civilization is redeemable. But if we are to further civilization, we'll need to implement a plan very soon. James Howard Kunstler, author of *The Long Emergency*, describes one such plan. In this essay, I augment his outline with some details and examples.

This is a not a 10-step plan in the usual sense; rather, we will have to start all of these steps simultaneously, and now. These steps are ginormous. That's a new word, as of 2007 when *Webster*'s declared it so. Interestingly, I read about it under a tiny headline. And I was quite disappointed that ginormous was chosen, but gihugic -- my personal favorite -- was not. In any event, here are the 10 steps:

<u>Step 1</u>: Expand our horizons beyond the question of how we will run the cars by means other than gasoline. The TechnoMessiah will not save us from ourselves, nor will she magically create a substitute for crude oil. The mainstream media would have you believe ethanol is the savior, when in fact the most likely outcome of the ethanol craze is that we'll use our gas tanks to burn through the last six inches of topsoil in America's breadbasket. Biodiesel represents the most viable of the alternative fuels, but it requires a choice: We can use our farmland to grow food, or we can use it to grow fuel for our cars. Given the choice between eating and driving, I suspect many Americans would choose driving. But cognitive dissonance runs so deep, they'll choose to drive to Burger King.

This obsession with keeping the cars running threatens our lives and our species. Cars are not part of the solution, whether they run on fossil fuels, moonshine, peanut oil, or buffalo chips. Rather, they are very clearly part of the problem, and a large part at that. It's time to abandon the car, time to make other arrangements for nearly all the common activities of daily life.

<u>Step 2</u>: We must produce food differently. Industrial agriculture is destined for disaster, and will leave in its wake sterile soils and an agricultural model at a grossly inappropriate scale. Within the next decade or so, small-scale farming will return to the center of American life. Think of the Victory Gardens of Oil War II as a small-scale, temporary experiment. Say goodbye to the 3,000-mile Caesar salad

to which we've become accustomed; say hello to locally grown food, recognizing that you might have to grow your own. In the near term, this situation presents many business and vocational opportunities for creative, hard-working people. First, though, we will have to retrieve considerable knowledge from the dustbin of history. And in arid regions, we'll need to obtain our water differently, too. When oil becomes too expensive or too limited in supply, we won't be using it to suck water from deep in the ground. In the absence of fossil fuels, the human carrying capacity of the Tucson basin, where I spent most of my academic career, is approximately zero.

Step 3: We must inhabit the terrain differently. The American suburbs and the interstate highway system are designed for a culture that has no future: the misguided car culture. The suburbs in particular represent perhaps the greatest misallocation of finite materials in the history of the world. Our suburbs essentially require us to live far from our places of work and play, and also far from all consumer goods, from food to furniture. We will have to learn to inhabit differently, or not inhabit at all, most areas currently dominated by asphalt, concrete, and tall buildings. These include, for example, Los Angeles, Las Vegas, and Tucson. Our cities must contract. Our towns must be re-inhabited and the areas around them must be re-structured to accommodate small farms and the manufacture of goods to serve the towns. This entire process will require gihugic demographic shifts and is likely to be turbulent. When the trucks stop bringing food and the water stops flowing through the taps and the diesel-powered trains are no longer bringing coal to the power plant; when all this is happening and the thermometer reads 105 degrees and the calendar says summer's not here yet; you'd better get along with your neighbors, especially the heavily armed ones who take a strict interpretation of the Second Amendment.

If you're looking for a job in the decades ahead, look no further than the brand-new fields of architecture, planning, and political leadership. The old versions of these enterprises are useless and must be abandoned. Consider our cities, as they currently stand: We have no sense of public space. Any small piece of beauty we might otherwise find between Wal-Mart and Target is obscured by the curvature of the earth. Our strip-malls are so ugly even winos won't hang out there. There's not enough Prozac in the world to make them seem nice. Are these places worth caring about? Are they worth defending? I'd guess there are at least 100,000 places not worth caring about in this country, and the number is growing. Actually, there might be 100,000 places not worth caring about in just about any major metropolitan area in the U.S. When we have more places *not* worth caring about than places that *are* worth caring about, perhaps that day will come that we'll run out of young people willing to spill their blood in the Middle East to defend our hyper-indulgent, nonnegotiable way of life. That'll be a dreadful day for American Empire, but a wonderful day for the rest of the planet.

Step 4: We must move people and things differently. You've probably seen the bumper sticker on about every fourth 18-wheeler on the interstate: "Without trucks, America stops." That's about right, at least with respect to economic growth. And the trucks are going to stop within the next few years. Shortly thereafter, the interstate highway system will simply collapse. Let's not waste our time trying to prop up our hallucinatory economy with its fatal dependency on cars and trucks. Rather, we could restore public transit. We could start with our railroads -- currently, we have a rail system the Bulgarians would be ashamed of -- and we could electrify our railways so they can run on solar panels and wind turbines. Then we could move to the waterways, starting by ripping out the condos and bike paths from the inner-city harbors and then restoring the piers and warehouses (not to mention the sleazy accommodations for sailors). Numerous career opportunities lie ahead for those hardy individuals willing to put away their iPods and Blackberries long enough to chart the course.

Step 5: We need to transform retail trade. The demise of Wal-Mart is at hand. Personally, I think that's a nice silver lining, albeit in a large bank of very dark clouds. The national chains have used inexpensive oil as the foundation for predatory economies of size, and therefore as the springboard for killing local economies. Cheap oil is fundamental to the 12,000-mile supply chain underlying the "warehouse on wheels" approach to the just-in-time delivery of cheap plastic crap. Don't think for a minute that Internet shopping will replace small, locally owned shops in every town: After all, Internet shopping relies on cheap delivery, and delivery will no longer be cheap in the days ahead. In addition, Internet shopping depends on reliable electric-power systems. Electricity is a short-lived luxury because all sources of power are derivatives of oil; for example it takes a lot of oil to rip coal out of the ground, and then a lot more to deliver it to the power plant; it takes a lot of oil to construct a solar panel or a wind turbine, or even to maintain dams used to generate hydroelectric power. Again, there are plenty of career opportunities for energetic individuals interested in small, local businesses. In the locally owned shops of the future, even the much maligned "middle man" will be making a comeback (so, too, will the lesser-known "middle woman").

Step 6: We have to start making things again. We will have far fewer choices when we go to the store, but we still will want clothes and household goods. We don't know how we're going to make things, or even what we're going to make, in part because we haven't made much of anything in this country for such a long time. But I'm counting on American ingenuity to light the way. If you're looking for a job, there's plenty that needs to be done because there's plenty that needs to be manufactured.

Step 7: We need artists again. When the power goes out, we won't get to decide between listening to Britney Spears and watching the latest rendition of *American Idol*. And people think I'm a pessimist! We're going to need playhouses and live performance halls, albeit without high-tech light and sound systems. And we'll need musicians and actors and playwrights and stagehands and theater managers. We'll need storytellers, too, to keep history alive when the publishers stop printing books. Again, the Internet is unlikely to save on-demand canned entertainment if the power's on the fritz. We'll be able to look back on the Internet as a wonderful piece of technology, if only because it unmistakably disproved the old expression: "A million monkeys at a million typewriters could reproduce Shakespeare."

Step 8: We must reorganize the educational system. Yellow fleets of school buses are on their way out. We have invested heavily in centralized systems of primary and secondary school -- most recently and disastrously in the form of "No Child Left Behind" -- and we will undoubtedly continue to invest in that centralization at the expense of true education. Such investment will slow the transition to a reasonable system of education that perhaps will grow, in fits and starts, from the home-schooling movement. More good news: It seems we will not be stuck with a public school system focused on churning out automata to serve industry. The current system was described by Jules Henry in his 1963 classic, *Culture Against Man*: "School is indeed training for later life not because it teaches the 3 Rs (more or less), but because it instills the essential cultural nightmare fear of failure, envy of success, and absurdity." Henry's scathing critique correctly pointed out that public schools eviscerate individuality and creativity, and therefore serve corporate America at the expense of Americans. The demise of corporate America will solve that problem.

I suspect higher education is doomed to fail for myriad reasons, including terminal indifference of the academy to societal needs. But if you can write a coherent paragraph and do long division, you can already out-perform most college graduates. If you can teach youngsters to do these things, I suspect you have a bright future as a teacher in a post-carbon world.

Step 9: Our medical system must be completely reorganized. Without power-hungry high-tech tools, we'll need real doctors again: people who understand how the body actually functions. In the coming barter economy, they'll likely make house calls to work for a meal or a place to sleep. On the other hand, we'll all be eating less and exercising more, so my doctor will be happy about that. All in all, there will be less concern about blood pressure, cholesterol, and various pulmonary conditions.

Step 10: Our entire socio-economic and political system will become much more local. *Every large system will fail*. If you can find a way to do something practical and useful on a smaller scale than it is currently being done, you are likely to be well fed and even revered in your local community. Local politics will assume increasing importance as first the federal government, then the state government, simply fade from relevance. Neo-conservatism clings tenuously to life but, much to the dismay of Business Party I and Business Party II, will soon be dead. The collapse of American Empire will bring many opportunities for local heroes. I can imagine one possible exception, one large system that may not collapse as we enter the new Dark Age: the Church. Because religions deal in the transport of ideology, rather than Wheaties and widgets, I fear they might assume the same power they did during the last Dark Age. I fear the rise of the Church not because I am opposed to other peoples' spirituality, but because I believe the problems we face can be solved only with secular approaches, not with wishful thinking. That stated, the worst possible outcome would be a battle to the death in a game of Last Man Standing. Our focus on the common good precludes a mentality of Us vs. Them; with the common good, there is no "Them."

There you have it: a thumbnail sketch of the agenda for those who believe western civilization is worth saving. I'm sure I've left out many important items, but take heart: any number can play, and there is much to be done.

Before you race to further civilization, please read the remainder of this essay. It's a trenchant reminder that civilization has its disadvantages.

Civilization requires hierarchy and oppression. As a result, it requires armed force. A recent Christmas card was filled with proud stories of the kids in the U.S. Army, and it closed with, "We pray for peace." I didn't know whether to laugh or cry. I'll skip the rant about celebrating Christ and mass, the two components of Christ's mass (i.e., Christmas) in which I don't believe, much less celebrate. And, too, I'll forgo the equally tempting rant about a religious holiday that promotes conspicuous consumption in an empire founded on secular ideals.

Never mind that the writer almost certainly is fooling herself. If her prayers are answered, that'll put the battle-ready kids out of their jobs. And, since war comprises the foundation for our entire industrial economy, the empire almost surely would sink to the bottom of the already stinking swamp within weeks of an outbreak of peace. Praying for peace makes as much sense as supporting the troops, and both cases of wishful thinking are clothed in lies.

Support the troops. It's the rallying cry of an entire nation. It's the slogan pasted on half the bumpers in the country.

Supporting the troops is pledging your support for the empire. Supporting the troops supports the occupation of sovereign nations because might makes right. Supporting the troops supports wanton murder of women and children throughout the world. And men, too. Supporting the troops supports obedience at home and oppression abroad. Supporting the troops throws away every ideal on which this country allegedly is founded. Supporting the troops supports the ongoing destruction of the living planet in the name of economic growth. Supporting the troops therefore hastens our extinction in exchange for a few dollars. Supporting the troops means caving in to Woodrow Wilson's neo-liberal agenda, albeit cloaked as contemporary neo-conservatism (cf. hope and change). Supporting the troops trumpets power as freedom and fascism as democracy.

Perhaps most importantly, supporting the troops means giving up on resistance. Resistance is all we have, and all we've ever had. We say we're mad as hell and we claim we're not going to take it any more. But, sadly, we gave up on resistance of any kind years ago. After all, we might get in trouble. We might be incarcerated for protesting without a permit.

When jets from the nearby military base scream over the university campus, conversation stops, indoors and out. We pause awkwardly, stopped in mid-conversation. After the jets pass, in formation, an excuse often is articulated by the person with whom I'm visiting: "It's the sound of freedom."

My response never varies: "Sounds like oppression to me."

The ensuing silence is more awkward than the scream of the jet engines.

It's as if America's cultural revolution never happened. It's as if we never questioned the dominant paradigm in an empire run amok, as if we never experienced Woodstock and the Summer of Love, bra-burning hippies and war-torn teenagers, Rosa Parks and the Cuyahoga River. We're right back in the 1950s, swimming in culture's main stream instead of questioning, resisting, and protesting.

In a Tucson coffee shop during the spring of 2011 I saw a woman, apparently in her early twenties, dressed in a short skirt, an apron, and high heels. Had she been behind the counter, she would have been the perfect symbol of the 1950s, a refugee from two generations gone by. We've moved from the unquestioning automatons of Aldous Huxley and George Orwell to the firebrands of a radical counter-cultural worldview and back again. A generational sea change swept us from post-war "liberators" drunk on early 1950s propaganda to revolutionaries willing to take risks in defense of late 1960s ideals. The revolution gained steam through the 1970s, but lost its way when the U.S. industrial economy hit the speed bump of domestic peak oil. The Carter Doctrine -- the world's oil belongs to us -- coupled with Ronald Reagan's soothing pack of lies, was the perfect match to our middle-aged comfort, so we abandoned the noble ideals of earlier days for another dose of palliative propaganda. Three decades later, we've swallowed so much Soma we couldn't find a hint of revolution in Karl Marx's *Communist Manifesto*.

In short, the pillars of social justice and environmental protection rose from the cesspool of ignorance to become shining lights for an entire generation. And then we let them fall back into the swamp. The very notion that *others* matter -- much less that those *others* are worth fighting for -- has been relegated to the dustbin of history.

The problem with being a martyr: You have to die for the cause. And along the way, you'll probably be jailed and tortured. But there's a fate far worse than being a martyr, in the minds of America's youth. There's the thought you'll be viewed as an anti-American freak, out of touch with Lady Gaga and *Dancing With The Stars*. A fate worse than death: Your Facebook page will be removed, thus "disappearing" you.

A line from Eugene Debs, five-time candidate of the Socialist party for U.S. president, comes to mind: "While there is a lower class I am in it, while there is a criminal element I am of it; while there is a soul in prison, I am not free." He was serious. So am I. That I am not taken seriously in these most serious of days shatters my ego. That Debs is not taken seriously these days shatters my heart.

When I visit with college-age people these days, they have no idea what I mean, and they believe Debs and I are misguided jokers. Completely immersed in a culture of make believe, mind-fucked from birth by the corporations running the media, the thought of resistance is, quite simply, beyond the pale. Resistance? Against what? And why? Isn't resistance a form of terrorism?

Every revolution has failed. And if that's not sufficient reason to launch a revolution, I don't know what is. The revolution is dead: Viva la revolution!

If any one of those troops we *claim* to support attempts to bring transparency and reform to this country, we instantly turn on him and support his torture by -- you guessed it -- the troops. Witness Bradley Manning of Wikileaks fame for a recent example. And who's the commander in chief of these troops? That's right, the man who promised transparency and reform, but who now seeks to crush the very people trying to bring it to us.

If obliterating transparency means criminalizing journalism, as the U.S. government is attempting in its flimsy case against Wikileaks star Julian Assange, we can live with that. Those journalists are probably terrorists anyway. Or worse, liberals. The First Amendment was shredded by Obama's predecessor, and how it's being turned to ash. The U.S. Constitution and Bill of Rights are bobbing along the same waves as social justice and environmental protection, sold down the river by a nation addicted to growth for the sake of growth (the ideology of a cancer cell).

It seems very little matters to the typical American beyond economic growth. And for that, most importantly, we need an uninterrupted supply of crude oil. All wars are resource wars, and even our involvement in the last "Good War" was about oil, notwithstanding revisionist history about our compassion regarding Hitler's final solution. Crude oil's near-term annual decline rate of ten percent, as suggested by Mohammad-Ali Khatibi, Iran's OPEC Governor, means many troops will be needed to secure the lifeblood of the industrial economy. After all, world demand hasn't peaked yet, although world supply has. If we're to continue ruining the world, we'll need plenty of troops. And they'll need your support.

Meanwhile, you keep supporting the troops, and trying to convince yourself you're fighting terrorism in the process. If doubt creeps in, turn on the television. Listen to the news anchors and the politicians, the characters and the commercials. Immerse yourself in the ultimate hallucination. Keep lapping up the self-censored "news," confident the future will bring even more self-indulgent hedonism than the recent past.

And if somebody tries to tell you the hegemony of the U.S. dollar is threatened, thereby causing the price of oil to skyrocket, you just ignore the uncomfortable news, just as the mainstream media have ignored it. That kind of thing can't happen here. It's never happened, so it can't happen (as described by Francis Bacon in his *Idol of the Den*). If some misinformed fool attempts to point out the consequences of consumerism, shrug him off as a terrorist. And if somebody tries to confuse your happy holidays by telling you the good news about economic collapse, you tell him you'll be praying for peace. That'll make it all okay.

Scale

During late summer 2009, I drove from Tucson, Arizona to the mud hut, taking a circuitous route through most of the Midwestern U.S. Along with my spouse and dog, I covered 4,200 miles while crisscrossing 11 states and all 4 time zones in the continental U.S. We circumambulated Kansas, and at one point we drove close enough to spit on the state. But it didn't seem worth the time or the saliva.

We drove slowly and stopped often, primarily because the U.S. presidential administrations' Keynesian approach to saving the industrial economy necessitates throwing money at the highway departments of every state in the country. The attendant "shovel-ready projects" are clear examples of the lengths to which industrial humans will go to sustain the unsustainable, maintain the immaterial, and generally restore the irredeemable for a few more months.

The many miles and frequent pauses reveal to any sentient animal the sheer lunacy of the living arrangements we've built for ourselves. Within the span of a couple generations, we abandoned a durable, finely textured, life-affirming set of living arrangements characterized by self-sufficient family farms intermixed with small towns that provided commerce, services, and culture. Worse yet, we traded that model for a coarse-scaled arrangement wholly dependent on ready access to cheap fossil fuels. Then we ratcheted up the madness to rely on businesses that use, almost exclusively, a warehouse-on-wheels approach to just-in-time delivery of unnecessary devices designed for rapid obsolescence and disposal.

Simply ingenious, wouldn't you say?

The entire region, formerly abundant with a multitude of edible crops, currently is brimming with a single commodity: #2 corn. It's Roundup-ready, at that, just to throw a bucket of insulting acid into the face of reason. Roundup-resistant weeds are popping up throughout the region as we bring Farmageddon to the heartland and eventually to the world. Most of the corn, which is essentially inedible until it is processed (i.e., pummeled with inordinate quantities of fossil fuels), is watered with the last remaining drops of the Ogallala aquifer, brought to the surface with the same finite fluid used to power our trucks and cars. Verdant fields of ethanol dreams are interrupted occasionally by a field of soybeans; without rotations of legumes, the soil would be so depleted of nitrogen by king corn, it wouldn't support even the great corn desert. The corn fills our bellies with death-inducing faux sugar. But we willingly trade some of that "food" for fuel because the associated dependence on automobiles allows us to burn off the final inches of life-giving topsoil to promote our culture of death in rapid-transit, individualized death-traps. Who could pass up a deal like that?

I'd like to spend a few minutes describing a small, but important, part of this big picture: food, and how we obtain it. Evolution of the genus *Homo* occurred about 2 million years ago (i.e., there have been about 100,000 generations of "humans"). For about 2 million years, essentially all food was acquired via hunting and gathering, which required individuals to work a few hours each week. Every member of every group had knowledge of, and respect for, the landbase. Life was "sustainable" (i.e., durable) for the relatively small populations of people in each tribe. Local sources of food met all nutritional requirements throughout the seasons, as indicated by persistence of groups for 100,000 generations.

Fast-forward 1.7 million years: *Homo sapiens sapiens* (i.e., the wise apes) arose about 300,000 years ago (i.e., there have been about15,000 generations of our species). During this time, essentially all food was acquired via hunting and gathering, which required individuals to work a few hours each week. Every member of every group had knowledge of, and respect for, the landbase. Life was "sustainable" for the relatively small populations of people in each tribe. Local sources of food met all nutritional requirements throughout the seasons, as indicated by persistence of groups for 15,000 generations.

Fast-forward again, this time only about 300,000 years, to the development of agriculture a mere few thousand years ago (i.e., less than one half of one percent of the time humans have occupied the planet and less than three percent of the span of the "wise" apes). This event is documented in the biblical book of Genesis. The Fall was a transition to farming, from hunting and gathering (and to a lesser extent, gardening). This event led to specialization, perhaps most importantly including separation of work by gender. It also led to the storing of grains, and therefore large cities and empires (Cain founded the first real city). As such, agriculture led us away from an egalitarian existence to societies characterized by huge disparities in wealth. Much later, and quite briefly, it led to a middle class.

At this point, deep into the industrial age, we have four disparate models from which to choose (although I strongly suspect the political and financial elite will not actually allow us to choose):

1. Status quo, which is neither desirable nor sustainable. But this is the option we "choose" with every politician we elect and every purchase we make. I suspect this approach is not viable beyond a very few years because of the ongoing collapse of the industrial economy. In the wake of economic collapse, we will access to too few fossil fuels to sustain this model, which has never been sustainable.

2. Agrarian society in which we voluntarily return to a finely textured, life-affirming set of living arrangements characterized by self-sufficient family farms intermixed with small towns that provide opportunities for commerce, services, and culture. This approach will require us to immediately abandon large cities en masse, train 50 million additional farmers to support the 300 million mouths we currently need to feed, and return to a hard-working, close-to-Earth way of life. It also will require us to immediately cease almost all travel, for "business" or pleasure, therefore conserving precious fossil fuels for the business of feeding our children. I can imagine a hundred or so people in this country would vote for this model, if we were allowed to vote for such things.

3. Voluntarily return to an egalitarian hunter-gatherer existence. I don't think a dozen people in this country would join me in voting for this model.

4. Let reality send us to the egalitarian hunter-gatherer existence. I'm guessing we'll let reality do the trick because our hubris won't allow a willing transition back to anarcho-primitivism. This is likely to occur far sooner than most people believe, because the ongoing collapse of the world's industrial economy will be complete quite soon.

The collapse of the industrial economy will pose significant challenges because we have lost almost all the knowledge needed to forage locally. In addition, that knowledge is a moving target: Ongoing global climate change already is changing the distribution and abundance of plants and animals, and this trend is accelerating with every tank of gas we burn into the atmosphere.

Back on the road, obnoxiously ubiquitous cell-phone towers line the edges of the cornfields adjacent to the Eisenhower Interstate Highway System ("Celebrating 50 Years, 1956-2006"). Each of these completely unnecessary towers of mortality -- which serve only to duplicate extant infrastructure -- kills several thousand birds each year. Yet every imperialist has a cell phone, regardless of the death to songbirds. Don't even get me started on the col-tan mined from the Congo for cell-phone batteries, because I'd rather not think about the brutal lives and tortuous deaths of the Congolese women and children we treat as collateral damage along our imperial path.

Seemingly every tenth cell-phone tower marks a casino, yet another ubiquitous structure we'd be far better off without. These businesses extract money from the poor as they pursue the something-for-nothing goal upon which our culture has become based during the last few decades.

If it's not a casino, it's a distribution center for this country's rapidly waning commercial sector. We no longer make much of anything in this country, but we move around ton after ton of cheap plastic crap to the Targets and Wal-Marts that have displaced family owned businesses in every town and city in the country while exporting disaster capitalism throughout the world.

Finally, then, we come to the most ludicrous part of the entire endeavor: suburbia, filled with McMansions. This not-quite-country, not-quite-city living arrangement requires people to buy one of everything for every house -- except cars, of which we need at least two -- to live far from work, far from play, and far from the things we "need" to buy. Hundreds of acres of shoddily constructed, castle-like symbols of self-indulgence are separated from equally coarse-scaled places we use to grow "food," conduct "commerce" in our "service"

141

economy, and otherwise live civilized lives. As has often been the case, today's symbols of gluttony are tomorrow's death traps.

As usual, I'm quick to point out the silver lining in this otherwise disastrous narrative: Better days lie ahead. How could they not?

In the near future, we'll return to a durable set of living arrangements. Since we need about 50 million additional gardeners to support the 300 million people in this nation, and because nearly everybody in the industrialized world would rather push electrons in a cube farm than push a shovel in a garden, I don't foresee us voluntarily returning to the agrarian age. Not only are a majority of people unaware of the predicament we face -- thanks to the media, every level of government, and our own self-absorbed preference for the bliss of ignorance -- but there's simply no leadership in the industrialized world as we face an inevitable but unprecedented economic contraction. As a result, I suspect we'll bypass agricultural pursuits and plunge right back to the post-industrial Stone Age. Once again, daily life will be characterized by a finely textured, life-affirming, durable set of arrangements characterized by respect for each other and reverence for the land, and accompanied by a solid dose of self-sufficiency.

The point of my circuitous route to the mud hut: a wedding on the in-law side of the family. The newlyweds are twenty-something Army officers, and the event fittingly provided the perfect example of the malevolence needed to maintain civilization. Held in a venue designed and constructed to celebrate American military prowess (the Kalamazoo Air Zoo), the reception allowed the guests to enjoy flight simulators between bouts of gorging on meat, fat, sugar, and alcohol. Each of us was allowed to "fly" a fighter jet and blast the enemy. I was a tad disappointed, though: I didn't get to bomb a children's hospital in the name of bringing democracy to a poverty-stricken, oil-rich country.

For those readers who would like to impress upon me that I'm an imperialist, too, or that "freedom isn't free," don't bother. In a heartbeat, I'd give up every aspect of the industrial economy, even if it cost me my life, to know western civilization was dead and gone. And for those who believe we're really free, take a look around. See the security cameras. Notice the listening devices. Pay attention to the monitoring devices that record and report every transaction you complete. These tyrannies are among the thousands of minor costs we pay for "freedom" from terrorists (aka freedom fighters). The larger costs are borne by non-human species and people in non-industrial cultures every minute of every day.

I took a break from the festivities to spend a little time outdoors as darkness was falling. In a few minutes, I was able to observe far more beauty than marked the cultural ceremony or the route along the way: the cry of a red-tailed hawk drew my eye to two hawks flying low over the treetops. Shortly afterward, a brilliant harvest moon scaled the eastern horizon.

Hope springs eternal in, and from, the natural world: There's still something worth saving from the ravages of civilization. But is there world enough, and time? And, despite mounting evidence to the contrary, are there enough of us who actually care about saving the living planet?

Preparing for collapse: a personal example

I love the Socratic aspect of academia, and it's the part I do best. I supervised nine independent-study projects during my final semester at the University of Arizona, with a total of ten students. Most of them spent a weekend at the mud hut. One of the students, the poet in residence at the renowned University of Arizona Poetry Center, called the visit "transformative." I met regularly with all the students, probing and pushing until they do more and better work than any of us thought possible. Ditto for the small, hard-working herd of graduate students I advised and mentored during two wonderful decades.

It's a good thing I love highly individualized projects, because my department head banned me from teaching in my own department as soon as she arrived, a couple years before I left academic life. One of her very first actions was to prevent me from teaching a class I created and then taught for ten years. Apparently students were learning all the wrong things. Instead of focusing narrowly on production of livestock and other amenities critical to human well-being, thereby training students for jobs, I was educating them to lead lives of excellence. As you can imagine, the university administration put a stop to that nonsense.

If you're keeping score, training is for dogs. Education is for scholars.

Then, of course, there is my scholarship, which has been reviled by my college dean and university president for years. A decade before I left the ivory tower, my open letter to the president appeared in the morning daily because he wouldn't respond to my individual requests. The headline got his attention ("UA should cherish Krutch garden, not move it") and helped save the final, tiny patch of desert in the center of campus from red pavers and fountains (the fountains, which were installed nearby, were turned off a few years after they were installed as a cost-cutting measure). The situation has since eroded, while spreading well beyond the university president. I just kept asking the hard, but obvious, questions and, in exchange, I kept getting kicked in the head. An exemplary exchange had me pointing out the dire state of our energy situation (albeit before it became apparent to the masses), to which my college dean responded in the same newspaper with, "he's not one of us," and I forced him to admit his error with a lengthy piece I ghost-wrote for him (in return, I let him keep his job and I let the university keep money in their litigation coffers).

And finally, there was my embarrassing outreach, which involved teaching poetry at incarceration facilities (while also including a charter high school and a course I developed in the honors college). Imperialists would rather ignore important issues than address them in a constructive manner. And there's no denying the imperialism of typical administrators at any Research I university. Or, for that matter, the honesty and integrity of the typical inmate relative to the typical administrator. Why, the administrators plead, would I bother to work with criminals when I could be doing important work, such as justifying livestock on public lands and otherwise promoting imperial ambitions? Never mind that, in 2008, the United States became the first country in history to incarcerate more than one percent of its adult population. And it's working so well, wouldn't you say? By nearly every measure, we're spending more and getting less from our "justice" system than any other country.

Teaching? I was doing the best work of my life. Scholarship? Likewise. Outreach? Ditto. Obviously, it was time for me to move along.

I never thought I'd give in. I thought I'd be holding administrative feet to the proverbial fire, forcing deans, department heads, and presidents to do right until the whole thing fell down. *Illegitimi non carborundum*: It's been my rallying cry for 15 years, since one of my beloved graduate students explained the phrase to me (loosely interpreted, the Latin phrase translates to "don't let the bastards wear you down").

Alas, the bastards wore me down. And, finally, out. My last day on the taxpayer dime was 1 May 2009, twenty years to the day after I was hired. Fittingly, May Day is a day of celebration for labor and laborers throughout the world. My department accepted my resignation with considerable glee, and the university granted me emeritus status so I can keep working for free. Stunningly, they didn't offer a gold watch.

Perhaps I cut off my nose to spite my face. But, as my brother points out on his blog, that'll make it easier for me to stick my head up my butt. And I can assure you I'm terrified. As I abandon the ship of empire for my lifeboat, it's difficult to see anything but choppy seas between here and the distant horizon.

Now that I've made my choice, I couldn't be happier. And my physical health has benefitted, too.

Upon graduation from high school, I carried 165 pounds on my 6'1" frame. I was the epitome of skin and bones, lean from constant athletic events and the associated preparatory training. My red-hot metabolism probably had a lot to do with it, too.

During the hard-working summer of 2009, shortly after I left the cushy university life, I was working with a sense of urgency rooted in my strong suspicion the industrial age had nearly run its course. Back in Tucson after a back-breaking two weeks at the mud hut, I tracked down a scale. Sure enough, I was working entirely too hard. I'd added two inches to my height since high school, and a whopping three pounds. If I was skin and bones back in the day, I'm now 168 pounds of callused skin on degenerating bones.

Preparations at the mud hut increased rapidly during the summer of 2009, as did my own skills. When we started, I could barely distinguish a screwdriver from a zucchini. That's one price for an academic life that proceeded from high school to undergraduate school to graduate school to post-doc to first academic job to tenure-track position without taking a breath. I was a highly accomplished full professor by the time I hit forty, but I couldn't fix my cranky toilet or hang a door. If somebody as inept as me can develop trade skills, just about anybody else can, too.

And those skills developed quickly, with only minor injuries. Along with my similarly inept friends at the mud hut, I've developed ample infrastructure to provide food and water, and to maintain temperatures comfortable for us. Our goal is not merely to survive, but to thrive, during the post-carbon era.

The failure of leadership on the issue of energy decline and the associated economic collapse is comprehensive. If you think the government -- or anybody else for that matter -- will bail your sinking rowboat when civilization completes its decline, you failed to notice how long it took FEMA to get drinking water to the Superdome in the wake of Katrina. That was a temporary inconvenience, and the feds had access to plenty of resources, including carbon-based ones.

Disruptions in electrical power and the flood of food at the grocery store, not to mention disruptions in drinking water, pose a significant challenge to human survival. Thriving in this environment will require a certain set of psychological traits and some serious planning. I am often asked about the latter issue (apparently the perception that I'm insane precludes much inquiry about the former issue).

Preparations will be different for every person and every place. I live in the American Southwest, a region that presents huge obstacles to post-carbon survival. Due to familial issues, I'll be staying in the area until well after TSHTF, thus precluding my exit to a location more desirable to me (e.g., Belize, Hawaii's big island). Caveat emptor: The following description is relatively specific to the southwestern United States.

Regardless where you choose to spend your post-carbon years, a few things are necessary: water, food, shelter, and human community. Piecing together an existence that supplies each of these elements will not be easy, but I think creative people will be able construct a life worth living. A few people will even thrive, helped along by the knowledge that the collapse of American Empire is wonderful news for the many species and cultures with which we share the planet. I wish to be among those people, although I recognize the odds are long.

I'm not suggesting the transition has been easy for me, or that it will be easy for others who pursue such a route. Nonetheless, I am frequently told how easy life is for me, always by people who think life is difficult for them, as they go on to explain. According to these tortured souls, life is hard because they haven't made the necessary psychological commitment to the notion of a world economic collapse. And I have, so I have it easy.

I am certain of only one thing: Living rationally may have its rewards, but an "easy" life is not one of them. Yes, I made the psychological commitment to the obvious. And that part -- arguably the most important part of this whole affair -- was relatively easy, I suppose because life-long education in ecology makes me understand there are limits to growth. The Ph.D. minor in economics helped a little, if only to pull back the curtain to expose the flawed arguments of neo-classical economists.

But allow me to start with the bigger, more important issue, the one that actually threatens our species with extinction: I mourned for many months when I realized our species was likely to cause its own extinction via global climate change, and soon.

Imagine my elation when I discovered there is one potential, viable solution to this predicament. But when I point out that solution, I am not exactly hailed as the savior of our species. We studiously avoid even discussing that option, thereby committing ourselves to the aforementioned extinction. This is absurd and obscene, to me and nearly a dozen other people on the planet.

But, back to my elation, and the ease of my life in these economically challenging times.

Cheerleaders for empire (hence, to our own near-term extinction) go on to explain another source of my ease: I have no children, and they do, so they have so much more to worry about than simple-living me. As if I didn't make the choice about procreation, on my own. As did they. It was obvious to me, from the time I was twenty, that bringing more people into the world was not going to help the living planet or its human occupants. I decided not to contribute to planetary overshoot. Somehow, that makes me the self-absorbed bad guy.

And on they go, about the dreams they have for their children. Their children should be allowed to travel, as they did. The children should be allowed to experience the world's cultures (and fly safely back to the comforts of the empire). As if there are no costs to our addiction to fossil fuels. As if I don't have dreams of my own, which I'm unable to pursue. Through an entire career, I did what I was "supposed" to do: Nose to the grindstone, saving a majority of my earnings, I put my dreams on hold until after retirement. In other words, I threw it away, down the rat-hole of imperial dreams.

At some point, our dreams must match reality. Most people hate that. Sometimes, I'm among them.

Never mind the hard work, physical, mental, and emotional, I've invested in my post-carbon future. That's actually been fun and rewarding (and it'll be a lot more rewarding in the near future).

There's more. (Isn't there always?)

I love my family. But I doubt I'll know when my parents die. And I'm certain I'll not know when my siblings and their family members die.

When there's no food on the shelves, no gas at the convenience store, and no water coming out the municipal taps, it's safe to conclude the empire has abandoned you. But if you think an economic recovery is right around the corner, you still will not abandon the empire. By that time, it's too late to start thinking about other arrangements. Hell, it's too late to pack the car and hit the road.

I worry how hyper-indulged Americans will behave when the industrial economy completes its collapse. I fear American exceptionalism will turn quickly into exceptional ugliness toward one another.

Let me put it another way: If you believe clean water is a gawd-given right, and you believe "your" clean water originates at the tap, you'll defend to the death the system that allows (insures?) clean water coming out the tap. Unfortunately, very few Americans understand where their food and water actually come from.

Will we transform immediately and totally into ill-behaved rats, clustered in a cage without food? Perhaps, at least in the cages known as cities, particularly when the food runs out, along with the municipal water. But people in the "tribes" known as neighborhoods and communities will try to get along, at least for a while, at least while we're all suffering more-or-less equally. Small communities will be particularly well-suited for the hard times ahead. The neighborhoods of suburbia, on the other hand, are particularly poorly suited for neighborly behavior of the Mr. Rogers kind. Indeed, sprawling American suburbs seem to have been designed specifically for anonymity and therefore uncaring, unfriendly neighbors.

Which brings me to the mud hut, my personal refuge.

As I've intimated, it's quite rural. The nearest town of 10,000 is more than 30 miles away, the nearest real city 200 miles. Within a couple miles, there are 50 people, maybe 100. We're alongside a road to nowhere -- it ends a couple miles beyond our property, at a poorly maintained, little-used campground. We know the neighbors, and they know us. We get along, in large part because we're willing to help each other. And generosity is a trait we'll be using a lot in the near future.

Will we see marauding hordes in the months and years ahead? There's little doubt in my mind people will try to gather into groups and, playing grasshopper to my ant, attempt to take armed advantage of my advanced preparation. After all, the nearly perennial nearby river is reasonably well known by people in the region. And at least a few people know my thoughts on the matter, and are likely to try to find me and "mine."

On the other hand, people are likely to remain firmly entrenched in denial, at least while the revolution is televised. And every day in denial, wishing it'll all work out, is a day removed from being able to escape the deathtrap known as Suburbia, USA. By the time Joe and Jill Sixpack put the kids into the SUV and head for the wilderness they fear, lying beyond the city limits, it'll probably be too late to organize anything resembling a horde, marauding or otherwise.

So forget about Joe and Jill and their neighborly hordes. But what about Single Bill and his buddies? Well, maybe they'll get their collective shit in a sock, load up the truck with supplies and ammo, and make their way toward the mud hut. In fact, I'd bet on it.

I'd also bet we won't see any pitched battles in the front yard. Rather, I envision two scenarios. Either Bill and his buddies will employ the element of surprise and simply kill us, unannounced, or they will grab the very young youngster playing on the property and ask us to leave. Given a choice between the two, as if I have one, I'd take the latter over the former. Then, proverbial gun to the head, we'll leave. Quickly.

If we're so lucky, we must then ask the ecologically literate question, the one that should follow every significant decision made by humans: "And then what?"

Taking the property back entails an entirely different scenario than a pitched battle on the frontier. It requires planning, practice, and stealth. Needless to say, I've been working on the plan while trying to convince my neighbors about the importance of planning, practicing, and stealthing. None of this is much fun, for me or the neighbors.

With apologies for the self-indulgent nature of this essay, I have to ask: Easy? Compared to what, exactly?

In addition to threats to personal security, there are myriad details associated with staying alive when there's no water coming out the taps, no food at the local grocery store, and ambient temperatures are harmful to human health. How are we dealing with these issues?

Water is primary. Our landing zone has a river within a few hundred yards. The river is not quite perennial at the nearest stretch: it runs for 11 months, most years. The groundwater, at about 20 feet, is shallow enough for a hand-dug well. We took advantage of fossil fuels to drill a well, into which we installed a solar pump alongside a hand pump. The former draws water from near the bottom of the well, about 90 feet. The latter draws water from 45 feet. We have a water-delivery system, complete with ten frost-free hydrants and an extensive drip-irrigation system, to supply water throughout the 2.7 acres.

Food is a big deal, too. We're learning about wildcrafting (i.e., harvesting nature's bounty for our own selfish purposes). A neighbor harvests all his food this way. I grew up hunting and fishing, so I'm not averse to shooting and trapping animals for food. Our rural future offers opportunities for harvesting small game and the occasional deer. And we've started a relatively large garden in anticipation of the failure of large-scale agriculture. Remember, Eden was a garden, not a farm. We've stocked plenty of hand tools, and I keep asking for shovels as my birthdays approach.

We've put up a greenhouse and a couple of cold frames so we can get an early start on the growing season and to grow calcium-rich greens during the winter. We constructed a bee box and purchased a queen and workers, in an attempt to mitigate for the colony collapse disorder affecting honeybees in North America. We should be able to provide our own pollinators. We've constructed many garden beds underlain by hardware cloth to keep the gophers away. Each of the six dozen fruit and nut trees in the orchard gets the same level of protection.

A straw-bale chicken coop keeps the chickens insulated from the cold. The ducks are hardy, so they get along fine in a duck house without insulation. Collectively, the fowl produce nearly a dozen eggs each day, though I'm concerned about sources of protein for the birds during post-carbon winters. I built a fully insulated goat pen and goat run, and we're using the goat milk for drinking and as the basis for yogurt and several types of cheese. Already, we're well on our way to growing and preserving all our own food. In addition to making cheese, we're canning and drying foods, thus making excellent use of the greenhouse and wood-fired cook stove as we plan for a paucity of fresh vegetables during the winters ahead.

For food storage, we have two root cellars. One is surrounded by a block wall to keep it dry. The other has dirt walls to keep the humidity high. Between the two, we can store many different kinds of root vegetables and dry goods such as beans and canned produce.

For food preparation, we have an outdoor kitchen with a grinding mill and a wood-fired cook stove. Most meal preparation is done, at least in part, by our two solar ovens. We're taking advantage of ample sunshine in this area.

A small straw-bale house keeps the temperature comfortable for us via passive solar heating, geothermal cooling, and off-grid solar. We had the house built for us, using the money generated by selling our beloved home in the suburbs of Tucson. In a perfect world, we would have built it ourselves. But, although I can deconstruct ideas and talk all day about philosophy, government policy, and macroeconomics, I can't fix my cranky toilet. To say I'm mechanically disinclined would be a huge understatement.

I'm new to my community, so I am taking the time to get to know the neighbors. I'm attempting to inculcate -- and hopefully even endear -- myself into this community of a hundred or so decent, hardy folk, many of whom have spent the last few decades preparing for a low-carbon existence. Already, it is clear they willingly share their knowledge with those of us who are late to the party.

During the first couple of years at the mud hut, I dug trenches (requiring only a strong back and a weak mind, so it's the perfect job for me) in which to install water lines, and even installed frost-free hydrants throughout the property (I'm a plumber). I've laid tile atop a counter in the outdoor kitchen (I'm a mason). I've built several awnings for tools and shade, along with structures for goats, chickens, and ducks (I'm a rough carpenter). We're growing considerable food, planted from seed, in our own garden beds and also in a neighbor's field (I'm a sharecropper). My two favorite titles, then, are Professor Emeritus and Sharecropper. I never dreamed I'd have either title, back when I weighed a mere 165 pounds.

Going back to the land in the Age of Entitlement

During my youth, I was immersed in a culture of extraction and consumption. I was born in the heart of the Aryan nation in a small mining town in the panhandle of Idaho and I grew up in a tiny, redneck, back-woods logging town. Consumption was, and is, the prevailing culture in the United States. As with the extraction of ore and timber needed to support the unquestioned goal of economic growth, the consumption of materials and the costs associated with that consumption rarely are brought before the citizenry for critical evaluation. We live in the Age of Entitlement, assuming we deserve all we unquestioningly consume.

Although a majority of my school-age classmates denigrated education and wound up working in the mines or in the woods, I took a different route. Inspired by the words and examples of my parents -- both lifelong educators -- I vigorously pursued advancement through education, and completed a Ph.D. only nine years after I graduated from high school. Not surprisingly, my university degrees in forestry and range science focused on the production, extraction, and delivery of natural resources (i.e., destruction of every aspect of the living planet). Higher education led to a twenty-year career at a major research university, where my teaching and research focused initially on management of natural resources and, later, on a life of excellence.

During my final decade in the classroom, I took a strongly Socratic turn, asking my students how to pursue a life of excellence. Bound together as a corps of discovery in the classroom, we focused on the six questions Socrates found so relevant to the human condition and a life of excellence: What is courage? What is good? What is justice? What is moderation? What is piety? What is virtue?

Throughout my career in higher education, I nurtured the personal and professional growth of students and I questioned myriad aspects of contemporary American culture, typically via guest commentaries in various newspapers. Neither individual attention to students nor questions about culture were welcomed by university administrators, but my tenured status and international reputation for excellent scholarship allowed me to pursue the work I loved. In addition to writing numerous articles and books, I delivered about ten presentations each year to a wide range of audiences, from student anarchists to the U.S. Department of Defense.

Working at a major research university required me to live in a in a city, the very apex of empire. For years, I avoided the nagging voice in my head as it pointed out the horrific costs of imperial living: destruction of the living planet, obedience at home, and oppression abroad. Eventually, though, I could no longer ignore the powerful words of Arundhati Roy in her insightful 2001 book, *Power Politics*: "The trouble is that once you see it, you can't unsee it. And once you've seen it, keeping quiet, saying nothing, becomes as political an act as speaking out. There's no innocence. Either way, you're accountable."

And then there's the philosophy of Camus, which reminds us about the absurdity of our existence as well as finding worth in the act of rebellion. Rebellion cannot be meaningfully pursued while one is shackled to an imperial institution.

I departed university life for many reasons, among them to dedicate more time informing the world's citizens about the consequences of the way we live. My message centers on the twin sides of the fossil-fuel coin: global climate change and energy decline (commonly known as "peak oil"). After all, the most important race in the history of humanity is under way, although the world's governments and the mainstream media have failed to give notice. The world's climate is changing at an accelerating rate, with profound implications for nature and the humans who depend on the natural world. In addition, the world's energy supply is rapidly declining, which is leading to significant contraction of the world's industrial economy. These unprecedented phenomena impact every aspect of life on Earth, notably including our ability to protect the living planet on which we depend for our own survival. Time is not on our side.

If we continue with business as usual, we likely are committed to a 4 C rise in average global temperature by mid-century. Such a profound and rapid rise in global temperature will reduce, to near zero, human habitat on Earth. A reduction in greenhouse-gas emissions by at least eighty percent represents the single remaining hope to save the living planet on which we depend. Such a reduction in emissions of greenhouse gases will require either a near-term trip to the post-industrial Stone Age or a rapid accounting for the actual costs associated with consuming fossil fuels. The latter will require immediate recognition of the explicit links between environmental protection, social justice, and the human economy and therefore an unprecedented transition to physical economics. Either way, we're nearing the end of the Age of Entitlement and drawing inexorably closer to the Age of Consequences.

Although ecological forecasting is fraught with uncertainty, there is little doubt that some options have been permanently closed and others pose significant challenges in the years ahead. For example, long-term economic growth is precluded by inaccessibility to inexpensive sources of energy, and we are committed to at an average global temperature increase of at least 2 C. As I have written and said many times, dealing with the two sides of the fossil-fuel coin -- global climate change and reduced energy availability -- will require enormous courage, compassion, and creativity.

In addition to inspiration and motivation, we need practical, local solutions to mitigate for climate change and energy decline (it is too late for societal-level solutions to either predicament). Local solutions must be based on a realistic set of assumptions about climate and energy, and my message centers on the moral, philosophical, and pragmatic aspects of climate change and energy decline. My writing and presentations describe the nature of our predicaments, offer a series of assumptions based on forecasts for climate change and energy decline, give a general template for action, and then deliver a series of practical solutions within the realm of strengthening the links between environmental protection, social justice, and the human economy.

But, as should be obvious, I'm having damned little impact. I know exactly three people who, influenced by my message, have changed their lives in any way at all. I am one of them. The other two made minor changes in lifestyle when they began sharing their property with me. Considering how difficult it is to change ourselves, we shouldn't expect to be able to use words to change others.

At the height of a productive career characterized by frequent awards for teaching and research, my moral compass drove me away from the relative ease of a highly paid job in exchange for the joy of stewarding life in a small community. More than two decades after I started down the academic path that led to a productive career in the ivory tower -- and much to the amazement and criticism of my colleagues -- I returned to my rural roots to live in an off-grid, straw-bale house where I live off the detritus of empire as I practice my lifelong interest in durable living via organic gardening, raising small animals for eggs and milk, and working with members of my rural community.

I am fully aware that rural life has its benighted side. As you recall, I was only ten years old when a classmate aimed a rifle out his bedroom window at the base of my neck, an event that was hardly extraordinary in that time and place. But society has changed during the last forty years, and my new rural community is not as benighted as the community of my youth. We understand and appreciate diversity in various forms, and members of the community seek to emphasize the attributes that bring us together, rather than those that drive us apart.

As I look out the picture windows of the mud hut this overcast winter morning, snow-capped mountains in the nearby wilderness provide a stunning backdrop to the last few sandhill cranes in this small valley. The cranes are among the last to leave their winter home before heading north for an Idaho summer. They remind me that some things are worth supreme sacrifices. Some things are worth dying for, the living planet included.

It's not at all clear that my decision to abandon the empire was the right one. I suspect it will extend my life when the ongoing economic collapse is complete, and I know it is the morally appropriate decision (as if a dozen people in this country give a damn about morality). But Albert Einstein seems mistaken, at least in this case: "Setting an example is not the main means of influencing others, it is the only means."

My own example has generated plenty of scorn, but essentially no influence. On the other hand, the imperialism of living in the city and teaching at a university has rewards that extend well beyond the monetary realm. I miss working with young people every hour of every day. I miss comforting the downtrodden, notably in facilities of incarceration, every day. And I miss afflicting the comfortable, notably hard-hearted university administrators, at least weekly.

So here I sit, alternately staring at the screen of empire and staring out the window into timeless beauty. I contemplate the timing of imperial collapse and the implications for the tattered remains of the living planet. Half a century into an insignificant life seesawing between service and self-absorption, I wonder, as always, what to do. My heart, heavy as the unbroken clouds overhead, threatens to break when I think about what we've done in pursuit of progress.

Spring's resplendence lies ahead, with its promise of renewal. Is there world enough, and time? Will we yet find a way to destroy a lineage 45 million years old, or will the haunting call of the sandhill crane make it through the bottleneck of human industry?

A day in the life

Now that I'm retired from the academic life -- or rather, now that I've departed the academy in disgust and despair -- I no longer spend time in my swivel chair, dispensing information on the telephone or tending to the tender young psyche of an overwrought twenty-something. But there is no "typical" day, just as no two days were alike before I abandoned the hallowed halls. Nonetheless, in yet another round of egocentric, navel-gazing story-telling, here goes my attempt to describe a day in my new life at the mud hut.

After a fitful night filled with five hours of oft-interrupted sleep, I give up the painful prone position for the slightly less painful standing one. The sun is still behind the mountains, the sky gunmetal gray on this 37-degree spring morning. I flex my fingers, marveling at their nearly instantaneous transformation from thin and nimble to swollen and brittle, bend my back and neck as they compete for loudest and most frequent popping noises, and gobble a handful of aspirin to start the day.

After putting on my cleanest dirty shirt -- one never knows when a neighbor might drop by, after all -- I fire up the laptop, respond to a half-dozen email messages, and ignore the list of back-stretching and -strengthening exercises on the table. Maybe tomorrow, when I have more time. No, that won't work: I have visitors tomorrow and the next day, taking a quick tour of the property to view the arrangements we've made. The tea has been steeping while I read and respond, and now I drink it while plowing through a breakfast of cold cereal and piece of fresh fruit as I skim the morning's counterculture news and commentary. I peek over the computer screen as the sky turns pink, then azure, in the span of a few minutes.

Walking slowly to pick up the hay, I am reminded how pathetic was my attempt at construction on my first-ever awning. It keeps the hay dry, for now, but insufficient pitch and long-abused tin cause the roof to leak, thus prematurely rotting the boards. I carry the flake of alfalfa across the gravel driveway in a plastic "Tucson Recycles" bin, a reminder of my home city of twenty years.

I chuckle as I open the door to the goat pen, an old bed frame I found on the property. After placing the hay into the hand-made manger and filling the water buckets, I release Lillian and Ellie from the insulated goat shed I constructed. Lillian bleats anxiously, knowing she is about to get a quart of grain and relief from her full udder. Ellie, the barrel-shaped three-month-old kid, runs between and then jumps onto the straw bales in the small paddock.

Crossing the driveway, I step into the 15-year-old mobile home and check the temperature in the kitchen: 42 F, a few degrees warmer than outside. I arrange the quart jars, durable coffee filter, and funnel for easy pouring when I have a full bucket of milk, then grab the milking pail and wander back to Lillian. The aches and pains are giving way to an easy gait and appreciation for another beautifully verdant day.

I recall last week's visitors, a gaggle of university students. After talking for hours about economic collapse, including light's out in the empire and no water coming through the municipal taps, I was extolling the virtues of living in a "third-world" country with rainwater harvesting and hand-dug wells. A very fit, 20-year-old woman asked for clarification about the wells: "They really dig them by hand?"

I explained that I move as much dirt in an average weekend as required to dig a 20-foot well. Tears welled up, and she turned away.

Economic collapse is fun to talk about, until it becomes personal. And for most people, the personal nature of physical labor is no fun at all.

In the goat shed, I marvel at Lillian's calm disposition and take quick note of her condition. Her toenails need trimmed, so I'll get Carol to help with that when she comes back from a week-long visit to the northern half of the state. I marvel, too, at my ability and willingness to tend barnyard animals. I'm feeling good about my new skills despite the criticism from beyond the property. When my parents visited a few months ago, my dad -- a product of his culture, steeped in societal economic growth and individual financial success -- made a point to watch and comment: "I never thought one of my kids would be reduced to milking a goat."

Two quarts this morning, same as usual. It's stacking up in the fridge, so I'll make cheese tomorrow or the next day. I'm partial to Parmesan, but I'll check the inventory of hard cheeses in the root cellar to make sure we have similar amounts of Parmesan and cheddar. Chevre, mozzarella, and ricotta need to be eaten quickly, and I won't take time to cook a decent meal based on either of the latter two during the next week.

My mind wanders from the goats to literature. According to the Christian Bible, judgment day has us being divided into two groups of people. Sheep represent the good group, goats the bad.

As I've said for years, there are two kinds of people in the world: those who divide people into two groups, and those who don't.

In the Christian version of separating the people into flocks, sheep will reap the rewards of a life of servitude. Sheep go to church, pay their taxes, and watch television without questioning the messages of God or culture. Goats pay little attention to God or others. They're independent, intellectually curious beasts. The bible throws in several disparaging comments about goats and their habits.

Needless to say, I prefer goats. By all accounts, Jesus was a goat.

Here in the real world, goats are mischievous, curious, sociable, playful creatures. They welcome any opportunity to escape their pen, just to exhibit their intellect. They pull down anything we try to put out of their reach, and pull up what we try to pin down. As nearly as we can determine, ours like to play with the dogs and take evening walks down to the river.

Most of all, though, goats like to eat. Just as they try to dismember anything their hooves can reach, so too do they take a nibble of anything within range of their mouths. Shoestrings, shirttails, and buttons are fair game, along with rope and shadecloth. Among the results of edible food are two we particularly appreciate: goat milk and goat shit. The former is high-fat food, the latter is high-quality compost for the gardens.

Autumn typically is rain-free here. This year, we'll take advantage of the dry weather to harvest abundant poop from the goat pen and apply it directly to the then-recently harvested potato patch. Potatoes are heavy feeders, so the patch could use the nutrients. By the time we plant next spring, the compost will be working its magic. Nonetheless, we won't plant potatoes there, though we haven't decided which nitrogen-fixing plant to work into the rotation.

The other product from our goats is even more immediately rewarding, which better matches the American notion of instant gratification. We drink the milk raw (i.e., unpasteurized) and make a wide variety of cheeses. Goat milk is homogenized, so the cream does not float to the top. We have a cream separator with which to separate the cream, thus producing skim milk and the basis for butter and ice cream. We haven't yet used this device because we've been using any excess milk to make cheese.

Making cheese is so easy, even I can do it. Ingredients include milk, culture (we use cultured buttermilk or yogurt), a coagulant (we use commercially available rennet, but citrus juice, vinegar, or extracts from a few local plants will work) and, for some varieties, a little salt. The only necessary technologies are a cheese press and the ability to raise the temperature of milk to 120 F. We use a relatively inexpensive press, but you can make your own with little effort (although controlling the pressure is challenging in the absence of a specialty press).

The milk goes into the freezer for a couple hours as I let the ducks and chickens out of their respective houses. They'll range free all day, the ingenious ducks spending most of their time in the irrigation ditch adjacent to the property they discovered after living here only a year. As I gather the eggs, I take note of the trees and gardens on the east end of the property, including the paw paw trees I planted earlier this week. Back in the mobile home, I wash the nine eggs before storing them in the fridge on the shelf below the milk.

I water the seedlings in the garden. The carrots and peas are just emerging, so they need a light shower twice daily. The citrus trees seem to perk up every time I shower their leaves, so I hit them every time I walk past. Continuing to the west end of the property, I give a quick spray of water to the device I constructed for producing compost tea, open the greenhouse and cold frame, check the honeyberry shrubs

I planted yesterday, and briefly inspect dozens of fruit and nut trees in the orchard. The milk has been in the freezer for its required time, so I hurry back to move the chilled jars into the fridge. As I pass them by, the goats sing to me. The etymological root of the English word "tragedy" is the Greek word "tragōidía," which means goat song. So every time the goats cry to me as I pass them by, I say the same thing: "I know, I know. It's a tragedy."

They don't understand my humor. But the ducks laugh every time.

Today's big task is construction. The still-tender ribs I broke last month working on a similar project remind me to work deliberately as I attach an awning to the cargo container in the northwest corner of the property. We'll want to store bales of hay and straw and, when we can no longer obtain bales of either, stacks of hay from the peanuts in two large gardens. In time, peanuts will feed us and the goats, as well as improving the soil.

The frame is finished at 1:00 p.m., but only after I pummel my left thumb with a poorly aimed hammer several hundred times, walk back and forth between the stack of lumber and the new awning too many times to count, and nearly fall off the roof. I guess the ribs aren't a sufficient reminder. I'm thirsty, hot, and tired, and it's time for lunch and a phone call.

As I eat, I visit on the telephone for ninety minutes with somebody who follows my blog and wants advice about where to live. Earlier this week, it was career advice for a freshly minted Ph.D. and tomorrow's caller wants to discuss a strategy for telling her parents about peak oil. I harbor no illusions of having answers for any of these callers, and I know the customary caller is wise enough to seek advice beyond mine, but I appreciate any opportunity to discuss reality and how we can respond to it. I suspect my advice is overpriced, even at no charge.

A handful of aspirin later I'm back at the awning, misguided hammer in hand. After a surprisingly smooth afternoon characterized by few bruises and no blood, I complete the awning. I've covered the frame with plywood, tarpaper, and tin on an afternoon with temperatures in the mid-80s. Sweating and sore, I barely have time to hand-water the large garden behind the mobile home, trying not to notice how badly the beds need weeded, before my evening encounter with Lillian. Were Carol here today, the goats would have been walked a couple times, with special attention to the abundant weeds on the east end of the property.

Distracting Ellie with a little grain in her own bucket, I close the door to the goat shed and Lillian steps up on the stanchion I built to ease the milking operation. I apply bag balm after I finish milking her, give Ellie a pat on the head, and head to the mobile home to strain the milk into two more quart jars.

Supper is the same as lunch: rice and beans left over from last night's supper. A quick shower removes the first layer of grime before I put the goats into their lion-proof shed, lock the chickens into their skunk-proof coop, and herd the ducks into their raccoon-proof house. The setting sun sets the sky afire before unleashing the Milky Way.

One more round with the imperial screen of death allows me to catch up with a couple dozen email messages while viewing the latest dire news about the ecological collapse we're bringing to every corner of the globe. A cup of herbal tea to wash down more aspirin, a few pages of Nietzsche in the silence of the straw-bale house, and I tumble into bed. Sleep comes slowly and poorly, as it has since the summer of 1979 when I last logged six consecutive hours of sleep. Even then, my nagging subconscious was trying to tell me something about the empire wasn't quite right.

Sadly, it took me decades to figure out the problem. More sadly, most imperial Americans are well behind me on the learning curve.

As I descend into a fitful sleep, I ponder the alternatives available to individuals interested in thriving during the post-carbon era. The society we have come to know is doomed: Like global climate change, peak oil represents a predicament, not a problem. There is no politically viable solution to either of these great challenges. Political solutions require economic growth, forever, and therefore no significant sacrifice on the behalf of the electorate. Further, the industrial economy is underlain by the assumption of growth: The industrial economy grows or it dies.

As should be clear by now, we cannot grow the industrial economy while reducing use of energy. As a result, we cannot grow the economy while reducing greenhouse-gas emissions. Thus, we're stuck in a politically untenable situation: To save the living planet, including habitat for our own species, we need to shrink the industrial economy. But the industrial economy requires growth. Recent research indicates we need to shrink the industrial economy to oblivion to save our species. In other words, what we really need is to kill the industrial economy before it kills us. And by us, I mean all of us: the entire collection of wise apes. As a society, clearly we have made our choice. But as an individual, you can choose to the contrary, with benefits for your psyche and quite possibly your survival.

Crude oil is the master material, the energy source that provides access to all others. Economic growth requires ever-increasing supplies of crude oil. As availability of oil declines the price goes up (with considerable variability, as we have observed during the years since we passed the world oil peak in 2005) and the industrial economy starts to sputter. When the price gets high enough, long enough, the economy simply, finally, expires. The world has been on an undulating plateau of oil availability for several years, but that plateau leads to a cliff. According to the U.S. Department of Energy and the U.S. military's Joint Forces Command, the cliff comes before 2012.

I know no energy-literate person who thinks we'll be able to avoid the post-industrial Stone Age by 2025. Assuming a conservative four percent annual decline rate of crude oil between now and then indicates we will have access to the same amount of oil in 2025 as we did in 1970, when the planet held half as many people as it now does and the world was considerably less industrialized than it now is. And that's merely the gross rate of decline, whereas the net rate of decline will be much more rapid because it takes so much energy to extract and deliver energy. Oil priced a $147.27 per barrel nearly brought down the industrial economy a handful times I know about, and we're hardly out of the woods yet. There is little hope for the industrial era to persist more than a few years, and the next spike in the price of oil could very well be the trigger that brings the industrial era to a sudden close in an unprepared nation.

I suspect we'll pass through a new Dark Age en route to the post-industrial Stone Age. Indeed, many countries in the world are already there because they lack the world's reserve currency and the world's largest military. Bully for us: We have both, thus ensuring a steady supply of fossil-fuel-driven energy into every city and town in the United States. Well, so far.

As an aside, how long do you think we can maintain a military and a functioning industrial economy if we keep spending more than half our budget on the former? We could stop our involvement in wars, but that would be quite un-American, wouldn't it?

The costs of maintaining the nonnegotiable American way of life are huge, even beyond simple economics. The American suburbs are the antithesis of durable living, as they require us to live far from work, far from play, and far from the places we shop for disposable items in our throw-away culture. They require obedience at home and oppression abroad. American Empire is city living (i.e., civilized), writ large.

The relatively few people paying attention to the undercurrents of the industrial economy know the ship is taking on water faster than the governments can run the printing presses. As the industrial economy continues to lurch and stumble, the vaunted American consumer loses the ability to consume (in part because inflation is rampant on items that actually matter, notably including food). Because ours is a consumer culture, with personal consumption accounting for about two-thirds of the industrial economy, the ship is listing. The next financial crisis is already unfolding -- notwithstanding absurd reports from politicians, media, and the irrational exuberance, again, in the stock markets -- and governments have nearly exhausted their supply of tools to deal with economic issues. We hit the iceberg of peak oil and, as government administrators busily rearrange the deck chairs, it's time to launch the lifeboats, even if you believe consumption is a good thing. Personally, I think it's not, in part based on the definition:

Consume: 1. To do away with completely; destroy: 2a. To spend wastefully; squander: 2b. Use up: 3. To waste or burn away; perish

Consuming gives most people a temporary emotional "high." We're addicted to shopping. But I trust it's clear why rational people want no part of the consumer economy. If we cannot terminate the industrial economy, and soon, we'll exhaust all habitat for humans on Earth by the end of this century (and, if the models are to be believed, much sooner). Along the way, if we have our way, we'll destroy every non-industrial culture and every non-human species.

In the face of a contracting industrial economy and the knowledge we're headed for a situation with extremely limited access to fossil fuels, a quote from Peter Drucker comes to mind: "You can either take action, or you can hang back and hope for a miracle. Miracles are great, but they are so unpredictable."

What's an individual to do, in light of the imminent collapse of western civilization? In addition to hastening the collapse, some tools for which I describe briefly in a subsequent chapter (**Terminating the industrial economy: a moral act**), I describe four points along a continuum for your own, individual, post-carbon future: (1) transition towns, (2) agricultural anarchy, (3) hunting and gathering, and (4) traveling. Below I describe each approach, briefly, as a means of generating thought, action, and perhaps even discussion.

Transition towns allow us the fantasy of keeping the current omnicidal culture going, albeit in slightly different form. This model assumes a long descent that allows time for cities to develop alternative energy sources. Think solar on every rooftop, for starters, and gardens in every suburban lot. For this approach to work, though, the food shed must be sufficiently nearby and sufficiently productive to support all the people in the transition town. This seems hugely problematic in sprawling western cities, especially those with more than a few thousand people. And for areas with limited supplies of water, or water that is several hundred feet below the surface of the ground, it's difficult to imagine a scenario that doesn't include massive suffering along the way to a huge die-off. The inability to store energy in the absence of fossil fuels beyond a few years in expensive, transient,

167

and toxic batteries is a microscopic problem relative to the absence of ready access to water and food. And there's an additional problem with the transition-town notion: I seriously doubt we have access to the fossil fuels needed to create the needed infrastructure for the 250 million city-living Americans, much less the 3.5 billion people who occupy the world's cities. Solar panels and batteries simply won't make the grade -- there's not enough oil left to pull this one off.

When the lights go out in the city, chaos often erupts. Is your city different? If so, will that difference persist when the lights don't come back on, ever? I've often said and written that I would give my life to terminate the industrial economy, if only to alleviate the burden of oppression on the living world. I've no doubt, in fact, that I will make this sacrifice. And that's okay: My insignificant life pales in contrast to the living planet and the persistence of our species. On the other hand, although I loved city life, my city was not worth dying for. So I left to prepare, recognizing that fortune favors the prepared. In contrast, Michael Ruppert moved to his home city of Los Angeles with full knowledge L.A. would be among the first cities to go up in flames. Ruppert apparently was willing to die for the privilege of comforting the afflicted there, until he changed his mind a couple years later and moved to a "lifeboat" in northern California.

Agricultural anarchy was offered as a model by Thomas Jefferson, and Monticello was the prime example before it became a museum. Contemporary examples are found in nearly every "third-world" country. A large proportion of the towns and cities in Central America and South America never have had ready access to abundant fossil fuels. As a result, communities have communal water sources and people dig shallow wells and harvest rain from rooftops. On a daily basis, local markets are filled with fresh food brought from nearby gardens and farms. The power goes out frequently, and nobody seems to mind because the towns and cities are actually located in livable areas in the absence of fossil fuels to heat or cool every building (cf. Tucson, Arizona). In short, agriculture has always been, and still is, at the center of everyday life.

Hunting and gathering will doubtless make a comeback for a very few hardy, quick-witted folks. This model resembles the prior Stone Age, and clearly is the most durable approach. It worked for the first two million years of the human experience, and we fled from it as recently as a few thousand years ago. But if you can't find a tribe to go along, you'll be as lonely as a Saguaro cactus on an ice floe.

Finally, individuals can largely avoid the ravages of collapse by traveling from spot to spot. History has been kind to travelers because people rooted in a particular place hunger for knowledge. If you're to pursue this route, you'll need to be quick-witted, good-humored, and willing to lend a hand when needed. Also, you'll need to recognize and avoid danger. Traveling will be terrifying, but no worse than staying in one location. And you'll get to see the world and live an adventure-filled life, just as promised by U.S. military recruiters.

None of these options offer a life similar to the one you've known. But a different life doesn't mean a worse life, especially if you give a rat's backside about anybody besides yourself. There will be plenty of opportunities to serve your community, as there always has been, in the months and years ahead. We'll be living closer to our neighbors and closer to the living planet that sustains us all. For those courageous, compassionate, and creative souls willing to live in the world rather than in a cubicle, life's about to get even more interesting. For the vast majority of industrial Americans, though, life is about to become miserable and surprisingly short.

When my medical doctor learned of my aspirin consumption during a routine annual exam, she expressed a bit too much disappointment for me in saying, "I'm surprised you aren't bleeding out in this examination room." I'm off the aspirin, living with the aches and pains of a physically challenging life.

HOPE

Terminating the industrial economy: a moral act

People often accuse me of inappropriate behavior because I propose terminating the industrial economy. Interestingly, nobody seems concerned about the morality of the big banks as they devise ways to profit from contraction of the industrial economy. Indeed, politicians routinely try to distance themselves from the few informed individuals who have a clue where we're headed.

But back to me -- my favorite subject, after all -- and the accusations of inappropriate behavior I attract, like snakes to the eggs of ground-nesting birds. People will die, they cry, purposely and studiously ignoring the millions of people and other animals killed every day by the industrial economy. They act as if the industrial economy is propped up by a solid foundation of love and world peace. It's all rainbows and butterflies, that good old industrial economy. A friend and neighbor, channeling Buddhism, claims she is taking right action by signing petitions to halt a dam on the nearby river and campaigning for Barack Obama. As if petitions or protests ever stopped anything the kings of industry wanted to construct. And don't even get me started on Wall Street's front man, the Trojan horse for big banks and the Pentagon, the prince of (Nobel) peace, the U.S. president whose war crimes surely match Henry Kissinger's by now.

People accuse me of inappropriate behavior because, in this increasingly postmodern world, we don't talk about right and wrong. Cultural sensitivities, you know. Not to mention cultural relativism. Call me insensitive -- I've been called worse, and my skin is thick -- but I claim there is right and wrong.

I'm way too postmodern to believe there is absolute right and wrong. I gave up that brand of religion years ago. But on specific issues, in particular circumstances, there is damned little gray. Even in the relatively broad example of industrial culture, there is plenty of black and white.

The definition I'll use is straight from my buddies Merriam and Webster. Moral: 1 **a**: of or relating to principles of right and wrong in behavior: ethical (moral judgments) **b**: expressing or teaching a conception of right behavior (a moral poem) **c**: conforming to a

173

standard of right behavior **d**: sanctioned by or operative on one's conscience or ethical judgment (a moral obligation) **e**: capable of right and wrong action (a moral agent)

There can be little doubt that a system that enslaves, tortures, and kills people is wrong. Industrial culture does all that with stunning efficiency. Big Energy poisons our water. Big Ag controls our seeds, hence our food. Big Pharm controls, through pharmaceuticals, the behavior of our children. Wall Street controls the flow of money. Big Ad controls the messages you receive every day. The criminally rich get richer through crime: that's how America works. Through it all, we think we're free.

In contrast to western civilization, I think a system is right -- and even just -- if it treats people alike and liberates them, thus giving them freedom to live unchained from the bonds of culture, politics, and a monetary system developed and implemented by others. I will not go down the road of oppression at the point of a gun or the blade of a bulldozer, but it's easy to extend the notion of enslavement-torture-death to entire peoples and the landbase. It's pretty clear I don't need to go down that road: We're so thoroughly disconnected from the land and from our neighbors that we no longer have a clue what happiness looks like, much less how we might bring some home.

What, about industrial culture, is wrong? Let's start with the morality of war criminals such as Barack Obama, who is merely following in the footsteps of civilized people such as Thomas Jefferson and George W. Bush in fucking the living planet and every non-industrial culture. Consider, for example, Obama's actions at the world's climate-change meetings: He takes the political way out, claiming victory even as the world recognized his (and therefore our) horrific failures. His actions remind me of the John Ralston Saul quote with which I commenced one of my recent books: "Never has failure been so ardently defended as though it were success."

In North America, we've been quashing terrorism in since 1492, and we just keep at it, pulverizing the planet while imprisoning and torturing anybody who gets in the way of civilization. We have a long a sordid history, and we keep doing it again, and again, and again.

And, in exchange for a comfortably miserable life marked by an equal mix of unhappiness and i-Pods, we tolerate anything to which our hand-picked leaders subject us. This entire, life-draining, life-sucking enterprise requires us to tell increasingly absurd lies and convince ourselves they are the truth. Fortunately, this requires little effort on our part because we are awash in cognitive dissonance as we swim in an ocean of cultural denial.

It is relatively easy to make a moral case in favor of pulverizing the lands and waters myriad other species need to survive. We merely need to convince ourselves we're not really part of nature. And, because of the aforementioned ocean, that's not a problem. But then there's the more difficult issue: the future of humanity. How do we justify the ongoing, ever-increasing destruction of the hanging-on-by-a-thread living planet, when we and future generations need the literal ocean to survive? How do we justify the murderous blob of economic growth in the name of baubles but at the cost of human life? Does that seem right? In destroying the living planet and all hope for future humans to occupy the planet, it hardly seems to me we are "expressing or teaching a conception of right behavior," while "conforming to a standard of right behavior."

Like the rest of us, scientists are eager to please the public, so they're trying to make the dire medicine increasingly sweet by ratcheting up the dumbing down of the bad news. Climate scientists even developed a Dow Jones Index for climate change, because everybody knows and cares about the Dow, whereas nobody gives a damn about the living planet and our likely near-term extinction.

Notwithstanding graphs that please the eye but fail to motivate action, it's probably too late to stop the frying of the planet unless we bring the industrial economy crashing to a very abrupt halt. Even conservative mainstream scientists admit that only complete collapse of the global industrial economy will save us from runaway greenhouse. Naturally, the definitive journal article on this subject was rejected by several journals -- even the scientific community can't handle this particular truth -- before it was published in *Climatic Change* in November 2009. We do not know how quickly we'll need

175

to terminate the industrial economy to save our species. If we did, we could spend that entire span arguing about the morality of bringing down the industrial machine of death. Since we don't, we need to act as if the matter is urgent, which, as it turns out, nicely matches the data on the topic.

I am increasingly convinced that the only moral choice at all is to bring down the industrial economy as quickly as possible, and by any means necessary. If that means destroying property, think about the destruction of lives caused by industrial culture. If the requisite means of halting industrial activity are violent, think about the violence and death caused by every civilized action. Using a cellular telephone is legal -- and even encouraged by industrial culture -- yet it kills women and children in the Congo. On the other hand, tearing down a cell-phone tower that kills thousands of birds every year and facilitates the death and torture of Congolese people is a criminal offense punishable by imprisonment. Because tearing down a cell-phone tower almost certainly represents an act of terrorism, it is punishable by suspension of habeas corpus, torture, and life in prison.

Short of violent and illegal acts, we have few options at our disposal. In fact, using all means at our disposal still leaves us a few thousand bricks shy of a full palette. It appears even our most "outrageous" actions pale in comparison to the scale of the problem we face. The bankers are in charge, regardless of the immoral actions they take. The limited power we have is slipping away faster than justice in our courtrooms.

What does all this mean for us, the people with no voice? Does it leave us moral choices? Does it indicate how we ought to live, in a world gone horribly awry while we were ensconced in the freak show?

I have little to offer here, other than boring pragmatic advice about self reliance and introspection. We should be investing in our neighbors, as has always been true. And those neighbors aren't just humans. They're animals and plants, soil and water. We need to protect and honor them as we do our own children. We need to harbor them from the ravages of war, and also from an economy built on war. We need to live outside the industrial economy and within the real world of honest work, honest play, simple pleasures, and paying the consequences of our daily actions. We need to abandon a political system that takes without giving, long after it abandoned us. At the most fundamental level, we need to re-structure society so that children understand and value the origins of food, and life.

It's no longer just the living planet we should be concerned about. It's us. The moral question, then: What are you going to do about it?

This question reminds me of that period in my life during which I gave up the idea of an omniscient universal designer (i.e., god). The discomfort was palpable and foreign. After all, I was relinquishing the certainty of eternal life with a loving god for a brief life filled with existential angst in a horrible place (or so I was led to believe by religious leaders). But, for me, reason prevailed. Once I saw the universe through a certain lens, there was no going back. Furthermore, the absurdity of my former life was -- and is -- a constant source of personal amusement.

In many ways, it's easier the second time around. I've given up on fantasy and committed myself to a life based on reason. But the pain is no less torturous and I feel even emptier this time around. There is simply no feeding the hollow spot in my gut and my psyche, as there was when I replaced my invisible, omnipotent friend in the sky with reason. Instead of abandoning the mirage of eternal life, I'm abandoning the mirage of globalization. Instead of giving up an ever-loving god, I'm giving up a comfortable life spent with my best friend. I'm taking yet another step in the path from make-believe to reality. And, as we all know, reality is a harsh, dispassionate mistress who doesn't give a damn about the emptiness in my fragile little psyche. Fortunately, I still have the amusing memories of the absurdity of my former life, in which I believed I was saving the world by conducting and publishing mundane research and teaching irrelevant concepts to a largely disinterested audience.

I found the first step to be the most difficult. Simply recognizing the industrial economy as an omnicidal imperial beast forced me to cross a threshold most people find far too formidable to attempt.

We've never been here as a species, much less as individuals. And every cultural message tells us we're wrong, that the industrial age will last forever, that justice and goodness will prevail over every enemy (i.e., terrorist), that progress is a one-way street to industrial nirvana, that the harbinger of hope will keep the oil coming and the cars running and the planes flying so we can all soak up the sun on a sandy beach any time we need a break from our tumultuous lives in the cube farms of empire.

The angst really started when I crossed the Rubicon of Denial. Now I know what it means to have a nonnegotiable way of life. It means we need to kill every non-industrial culture and every non-human species to keep the current game going. It means we need to live as a collective, the modern-day cybernetic automaton, never questioning culture's intent, or ours.

But there's no going back. Once you recognize the industrial economy is omnicidal, once you recognize the United States as the most evil empire in the history of the world, once you recognize that politicians are simply imperial tools in the ongoing economic mirage, there's simply no closing your eyes to the culture of death.

I recognize my accountability. I don't want to bring torture and suffering to humans and other animals. I don't want to destroy the living planet so a few humans can continue to live comfortably at the expense of every other culture and species on the planet. I don't want to be responsible for extinguishing habitat for humans on Earth.

Do you?

After taking the first step -- stepping away from industrial culture -- the steps don't get any easier. If the culture is killing us, other species, and future prospects of human life on Earth, do we have an obligation to terminate the industrial economy? If so, what does that mean? Do we risk imprisonment, torture, and early death to save the living planet for future generations of humans?

Parents obviously cannot risk imprisonment. Familial morality conflicts with planetary morality. But what if the living planet is your family? What if the longevity of your children depends completely on terminating the industrial economy? Both are undoubtedly certain:

the living planet is your family, though you likely do not recognize it as such, and the longevity of your children depends upon terminating the industrial economy in the very near future.

How will your children remember you? As an incarcerated terrorist (aka freedom fighter)? As an indifferent imperialist, ready to sacrifice the living planet for your 401(k)? How will we face our children after we've destroyed all habitat for humans on this planet? Or, to take a very short step, how will we face our children after we've failed to defend the living planet?

We can extend the parental excuse to every human on the planet. We all have people we love, and who love us. There are few people who live like hermits, and I don't think we can count on them to save us from the industrial economy.

Imagine the world without Patrick Henry and a few other freedom fighters ready to give up their lives in the name of a brighter future. Imagine if they'd have been pacifists, willing only to sign petitions and carry out boycotts. Give peace a chance? That's exactly what the industrialists want from us: a passive populace, addicted to television and politics as usual, so they can fleece us while destroying the living planet on which we all depend. We're Winnie the Pooh, in this old joke:

The Knight: How would you like to be my lackey?

Pooh: What's a lackey?

The Knight: That's someone who does what he's told, without question, and for NO pay.

Pooh: What's the catch?

Many people argue that the industrial age is coming to a close, so no further action is needed on our part. These people are seriously outnumbered by those who think the industrial age will never end. Both groups are imperial lackeys, unwilling to ensure a better future for humanity by taking courageous action.

Ultimately, all I'm asking is whether you will do something. There is plenty to do, and any number can play. Won't you join me?

Whack!

Whack! The soil, such as it is, gives way to my mattock.

What if I'm right? What if the industrial age comes to its overdue close, taking the love of my life with it? What if she's stuck in Tucson, unwilling or unable to escape when the taps run dry at the gas stations and, more importantly, in her rental house?

Whack! Twenty more blows, and I've got a row of soil -- scientists would call it "unsorted alluvium" -- loosened and ready for my long-handled shovel. Eight feet wide and a foot deep, it's more cobble than soil, with occasional thin layers of gravel, clay, and easy-digging sand.

It's got to end some time, even if it's a few years off. The next case of $150 oil, assuming we get there before the industrial economy falls into the abyss, will be brutal for an already over-stretched American consumer. Banks are falling like dominoes on a mule cart over the bumpy terrain of declining energy supplies. When will the lights go out? When will I lose all communication with my brother, sister, and parents?

Whack! Fifty more rows give way. I take a break to gulp water and breathe the country air. I hear the cackle of a chicken as she brags about laying an egg. The ducks laugh, at her and me. They always laugh, the perfect audience for my twisted sense of humor.

My dad spent his early years in a house without running water or electricity, and it looks like he'll live long enough to see the circle complete itself. When he was a kid, his mother declared she'd had enough of the uncivilized life. She was leaving, that very day. She wondered if anybody was going with her. They all went, of course, her husband and their pack of kids. My dad met my mom in college and they dated twice before deciding to get married. They were mere children when they had three children. Fifty-some years later, they're still in good shape, as sharp as ever. Life-long educators, they instilled in me the work ethic and curiosity that saved me from the oppression of ending up as poor as they were, when they were raising three youngsters in a backwoods, redneck logging town nearly two hours' drive from the nearest real grocery store.

Whack! The mattock bounces off a massive rock. I scratch and claw through leather gloves pocked with holes, finally tossing the stone onto a small pile of cobble I've remembered to create beside the large mounds of soil mixed with gravel and cobble.

I was a year ahead of my sister in school, and we attended the same high schools and then the same college. We've always been close, and our weekend talks on the telephone remind me of the many late-night conversations that led to our similar life paths and offbeat philosophies. During an intramural flag-football game, my brother and I went out of our way to beat up on her college-freshman boyfriend, for no apparent reason except familial protection. Later, she found it funny. At the time, not so much.

Whack! I'm too old for the empire to fall. My bruised and battered body hasn't taken this kind of physical punishment since two-a-day football practices in high school.

I played cornerback behind my brother's defensive end every game of my sophomore season in high school. We taunted the opposing quarterback to run the ball our way. He rarely did. On the offensive side of the ball, I still remember the two passes I threw to my brother during his senior season. I never expected to relieve the star quarterback during the regular season, but he hit a rough spot so I played a single series. I called my brother's number, of course. And I drilled him between the numbers, only to see him drop the ball. So I called his number again, and this time he made the difficult catch and the first down. We're still close, and we share the academic life, albeit in disparate institutions.

Whack! I've developed four rows of calluses on my hands. I can hardly bend my fingers each morning after a pained-wracked night of little sleep.

What if I'm wrong? It's happened a few thousand times before. What if I quit my easy, over-paid job only to see the empire last another decade? I can't bear the thought of missing out on daily interactions with students for ten years. And what if we keep killing every species and culture on the planet, and I have to read the news every day for a decade? I can't bear that thought, either. What if we keep the industrial machine running long enough to destroy habitat for humans within a generation, as it seems we will? Surely the southwestern desert will be among the most miserable locations to face the demise of our species. What if I continue to see my wife of more than a quarter century only a couple days each month? Is that any way to keep a marriage alive?

Whack! My back aches, as it has for months. My imperialist doctor says I shouldn't work so hard. But this is my job now, preparing for our post-carbon future. Or maybe it's just my future, sans spouse.

Another couple years would be great, from a personal perspective, but can the living planet handle it? Every day brings us closer to the edge of environmental collapse and runaway greenhouse. Here at the mud hut, we could use the time to figure out the garden and the goats. Not to mention seeing our families another time or two.

Am I that selfish? Am I willing to forgo habitat for all future human beings on the planet just so I can grow some potatoes?

Of course I am. I'm *Homo industrialis*, after all. I care about me, here, now. Hell with tomorrow, and all the tomorrows to come. And potatoes are damned good, as any Idahoan knows. I'm pretty certain the existential angst isn't worth living through, anyway, for any thoughtful person. And why should I care about the thoughtless ones?

Whack! My arms and legs burn with every swing of the mattock. A sandhill crane, one of the first to arrive this year, trumpets in the distance. Although biologists don't know why they've been arriving earlier every year, I'm betting they're not bringing good news on the climate-change front.

I shouldn't have sold our house in the suburbs, much less quit my easy job to prepare. My wife loved that house, and our life. I should have stuck it out with her, keeping my mouth shut and playing field biologist instead of social critic. Then, at least, we could die together. And she'd have been happy during these last several years. Me, too, at least compared to the emotional rollercoaster I've experienced as a result of the pain I've caused her.

Whack! Sweat saturates my clothing and even my gloves, staining my hands yellow. I can barely see through my sunglasses, the lenses filled with sweat pouring from my forehead. Not that this job requires any more visibility than brains.

I'm just not cut out for post-carbon living. I'm a career academic. What ever made me think I could live close to the land? It's fine in theory. But in practice it's a pain in the ... well, every part of my body, which clearly is not too big to fail. Never mind the relative paucity of friends in my new community, most notably including my best friend for the last three decades. I simply have neither the body nor the intellect to thrive here.

Whack! Best I keep whacking away. Thinking too much never did anybody any good. And where'd this self-indulgent crap come from, anyway? Onward, upward, through the self-induced fog.

Schopenhauer's question continues to haunt: How to get through a life not worth living? Make it worth living? That hardly seems an option at this point, given the lose-lose scenario I've managed to create for myself, and her. Take the Hemingway out? That certainly wouldn't help her. Not that I'd notice or, once I've left the planetary station, care.

Whack! Ah, self-indulgence. I'll bet there was damned little of it before the age of fossil fools. I can't imagine people, tribes, or societies would tolerate the self-absorption rampant in contemporary industrial humans.

A life of service was my answer when I served the empire. It was the answer inspired by the example of my parents, and followed by my siblings. It is the answer of my mentors and colleagues. It was easy to find, and apply, in my ivory-tower life. Whether I find it here, in time, remains to be seen.

Whack! A hundred rows or so, and the garden bed finally is hollowed out, ready for the hardware-cloth "basket" that lines the bottom and sides of the bed to protect the future garden from the present pocket gophers.

How will I serve this community? It's filled with doomers, many of whom have been growing their own food and organizing their lives around imperial collapse for decades. How do I fit? Or do I?

As the economic collapse rapidly accelerates, I've been thinking entirely too much about post-carbon living. Specifically, I've been contemplating my future role in my new community. How will I make a contribution, and therefore justify my continued presence? What will I call my vocation, in the years ahead?

As I mentally peruse the jobs I've held, and compare them to a world without fossil fuels, I find the challenge ahead a bit daunting. I started employment as an agricultural grunt. My first jobs, as a teenager in an agricultural area in the heart of the Aryan nation, fell into the category of hard labor. After future hay fields were cleared of timber, and then repeatedly plowed, I tossed sticks and rocks onto a wagon pulled by a slow-moving tractor. At the end of the day, covered from head to toe with several layers of fine agricultural soil, I had to be sprayed with a hose before my mother would allow me into the house. As I grew stronger, I moved up to bucking hay bales from field to truck and then from truck to barn. An over-developed work ethic made me quite good at both these jobs. But I no longer possess a teenager's body, and job prospects are not particularly bright for activities that require fossil fuels, including large-scale timber removal and large-scale agriculture.

My first "real" job was wildland firefighter for a state lands department. Specifically, I worked summers between my undergraduate semesters as member of a helitack crew, escorted by helicopter or truck to wildfires in a million-acre protection area. Again, my over-developed work ethic, matched with a competitive drive and an inability to sleep, made me damned good at this job. I could hike for hours with a heavy pack, and then pound the ground all day with a Pulaski. After a thirty-hour shift, I could sleep a couple hours and start all over again. But today, although I have the same inability to sleep, I lack the work ethic, competitive drive, and work-hardened body requisite for this job. There are other issues, too: I doubt we'll be seeing many functioning helicopters, trucks, or state lands departments in the years ahead.

During semesters on campus as an undergraduate student, I held several jobs, the most notable of which were night janitor in the student union and roofer on the university's indoor football stadium. I was a decent janitor, though my wife claims I've lost that ability. But I was a terrible construction worker. I kept dropping circular saws, thereby nearly killing my compatriots working below me on the huge roof, and I nearly killed myself when, too lazy to tie myself off as I was operating a nail gun halfway between the peak of the domed stadium and the ground, I tumbled, crashed, and collected an impressive rope burn on the ungloved hand holding my lifeline. Given the impending demise of large organizations, I don't have to worry about killing myself on large construction projects. But these experiences are sobering evidence that my future vocations are limited by lack of technical skill.

I've spent nearly my entire working life in the academy, which has made it clear that a career in the ivory tower is damned poor preparation for post-carbon living.

I suspect we'll be able to barter a little food, and maybe even some water from our hand-pumped well. We have an orchard, and presumably it'll produce some fruit. I suspect I'll be able to shoot the occasional deer or collared peccary (i.e., javelina), and therefore generate food and good will for my community. Perhaps, with our outdoor kitchen and abundant preparations, we'll be able to process the occasional morsel for the community.

Personally, I'd like to continue teaching, though I'm unconvinced my specialties will be much in demand. Conservation biology, anybody? How about philosophy? Or the history of pedagogy? Yeah, right. I can do long division, and I can put together the occasional coherent paragraph, so perhaps I'll be able to teach these skills in exchange for our many needs. Otherwise, I would seem to be relatively worthless to my community. I'm inclined to believe people who do not make themselves worthwhile will not be tolerated, once the days of economic growth cease and we can no longer support the traditional American lifestyle of carefree indulgence, replete as it is with free riders.

Like most people, I've long been interested in the notion of my legacy. Will anything I produce outlast me on this planet? Has my teaching inspired critical thought, appreciation for the natural world, or empathy for humans and other animals? Will the pages containing my written work be used for something other than fire-starter and toilet paper? Not that there's anything wrong with either, particularly in a pinch. After all, the pages are acid-free and therefore durable.

All of us reading these pages leave behind a depleted world. As we peer into the abyss of chaos, the world we are leaving future generations largely lacks potable surface water, abundant edible food, materials for constructing shelter, and soils for growing fibers. The stunning richness of species that greeted the industrial age has been replaced by a living planet barely hanging by a thread. As Derrick Jensen wrote in *Endgame*, forests greet us and deserts dog our heels.

At least we're leaving compost. I've come to appreciate compost quite a bit since I've launched my new career as organic gardener.

I've no doubt I'll be there in a few short years, corpse to compost, along with most other Americans. It is difficult for me to foresee a situation in which I would survive the completion of the ongoing collapse. Unlike most industrial humans, though, I will gladly make the ultimate sacrifice in exchange for bringing the industrial economy to its overdue close.

With respect to the living planet, I've placed my picket-pin in this small valley in the southwestern United States, former home to the Apache warrior Geronimo. Like a Cheyenne Dog Soldier, I've staked my terrain and will defend it from further insults. The nearby untamed river must remain wild, forever protected from industrial abuses and therefore able to support human life as we enter the post-industrial Stone Age. I've not yet achieved the expertise of one of my neighbors, who has spent the last couple decades sleeping outside, making fire with a fire bow, foraging wild foods, and drinking from the river. I doubt I will, either.

To ease the transition to the next Stone Age, we have created a durable set of living arrangements that will long outlast occupants of this property. Our infrastructure includes a house, hand pump, root cellars, and cooking devices that should persist at least a century, and probably much longer. I've little doubt these devices will outlast humans in this region, considering the dire nature of global -- and therefore regional and local -- climatic changes.

And then there's the big stuff, difficult to measure though it is. What about ideals? What about our sense of humanity? We strive to illustrate a style of living, unique to this time and place, which keeps us close to the land and close to our neighbors. Will it persist beyond my own generation? Obviously, I'd like to think so. But there's a problem with leaving a legacy: We don't know what it is or how long it will persist.

This issue reminds me of teaching. One never knows if the messages will be received, or in what form. For example, I taught my dog to whistle. She never did learn to whistle. But I taught with all my heart.

Will my legacy resemble my dog's ability whistle? Or will I get lucky and leave something durable and useful? Besides the compost, I mean.

Inmate wisdom

As my final semester on the university payroll wound down in the spring of 2009, I spent considerable time with friends and colleagues, reminiscing as we said our goodbyes. I was honored at many gatherings, none more poignant than my final day with the inmates at the county jail.

These men had been serving as advisors to teenagers in two other groups: Pima Vocational High School and the county juvenile detention facility. At the end of my last class in the Pima County jail, I wrote a poem to thank the inmates with whom I'd spent each Wednesday afternoon during the semester (they came to us from pods 2R and 2Q):

As we push away from the shore,
let us feel no remorse.
We have traveled so far,
though not always on course.
We are bound together now,
more *us* than me and you.
I will joyously remember
2R and 2Q.
As we cross the rubicon
and hear the door close,
another door opens,
filled with new highs and new lows.
You've been thoughtful advisors
to the kids and to me,
teaching through patience, kindness,
prose, and poetry.
Instead of mourning our goodbye,
our bittersweet ending,
let us not demand more, but instead
offer a prayer of thanksgiving.

It's easy to understand why I don't get paid for my poetry. In my ongoing attempts to link the arts and sciences, however, I agree with

188

the sentiments of Edward Abbey's 1977 book, *The Journey Home*. He writes about the intersection of science and poetry, but the message clearly applies to a broader interpretation of the arts: "Any good poet, on our age at least, must begin with the scientific view of the world; and any scientist worth listening to must be something of a poet, must possess the ability to communicate to the rest of us his sense of love and wonder and what his work discovers."

As I was reading my poem of thanks, my memory took me back to a day during the middle of the semester. To start us off that day, I read a short piece I had prepared for a forthcoming book about the end of cheap oil and the attendant consequences for American Empire: more of the good news, bad news of the twin sides of the fossil-fuel coin, with which the typical reader is well informed by now.

I didn't have to ask for reactions. As soon as I was finished reading, Zee (short for Cra-Zee) blurted out, "As a Christian, I believe Americans are chosen by God. We should use our military power to obtain oil and everything else we need." Zee went on to defend past and present abuses of American power because, after all, we need to maintain the way of life God gave us.

Sitting beside Zee was, as usual, Duster, who acquired his nickname with his ability, on short notice, to get his hands on PCP (i.e., phencyclidine, the street name for which is "dust"). As soon as Zee finished his rant about imperial Christianity, Duster responded with, "As a pagan, I believe we owe the other species and cultures on the planet the same opportunities we've had." Based on earlier visits, I knew Duster was quick-witted, and self-deprecating, and he was a proud anarchist and pagan. Duster went on to criticize past and present abuses of American power, cleverly and carefully trumping each of Zee's arguments with an effective counterargument. Zee fidgeted in his seat, his face reddening as Duster spoke.

Zee's retort was a vigorous, but poorly reasoned defense of Christianity, to Duster's amusement. Zee grew increasingly irritated, and Duster responded with ever-broader grins and shorter, more-frequent barbs. Duster was toying with Zee's emotions and exposing his flawed arguments, and he was clearly enjoying the experience. The tension mounted and the other inmates, most of whom supported Zee's Christian view, were paying rapt attention but not contributing to the debate.

I shot a glance at my co-teacher, a 19-year-old student who had enrolled in my honors course a year earlier and had subsequently immersed himself into *Poetry Inside/Out*. I could see Nick Jones' finger on the body alarm's red button, but I didn't think any of the inmates noticed. We'd never used the body alarm before -- in fact, we routinely joked about it, because we trusted the inmates more than we trusted the correctional officers -- but it seemed Nick was on the verge of calling the cavalry.

When Zee stopped to take a breath, Nick took advantage: "As an agnostic, I think we don't have much say in the matter." Nick was grinning as he parroted the earlier comments by Zee and Duster, and the room exploded in laughter. Immediately, another inmate added his two cents: "As a certifiable crazy man, I agree with Nick."

Madeline Kiser, the founder of *Poetry Inside/Out* and a dear friend who welcomed my involvement wth the program, finished turning the ship around: "What do you mean, certifiable?" The inmate explained that his legal classification was "incompetent but restorable." This was a good thing for him, because the legal system acknowledged that therapy could "restore" him to sanity, a classification that saved him from being institutionalized for the rest of his life.

As was customary, we wrote poetry as class wrapped up. Inspired by Duster's intelligent anarchy, I quickly penned this piece:

American the beautiful
America the powerful
Bountiful superpower
Malevolent hyperpower
We abandoned conservation
Necessitating occupation
Trapped by hypocrisy
One way out I can see
End the contradiction
Let anarchy ring.

Departing was such sweet sorrow, and I greatly miss interacting with incarcerated individuals (my current residence is 200 miles from the nearest incarceration facility). Unlike most people in mainstream American culture, inmates are willing to discuss important issues we face. These are people who speak truth, even to power. That's why they're there, at least in part.

The week after I left, Madeline solicited writing from the guys. Following the usual format, all the writing was completed in a few minutes at the end of a 90-minute, soul-baring class. I keep this example handy for those occasional nights I need emotional sustenance:

When people aren't around, and it seemed like no one cared,
I built up a lot of feelings I could no longer bear.
Was at my wit's end, and unsure what to do.
I signed up for a class and was no longer a fool:
a class that is different, a class that is new.
A class led by a man, a man who is cool.
I can see that he's smart in every which way.
I can see that because he changes lives every day.
Soon he'll be leaving us, but that's only in sight.
The things that he does, he'll continue the fight:
taking the bad out of people to make them feel good.
I know that he does it because he knows that he should.
    Going to miss him,
        By a soul he touched.

As I break away from the shores of American Empire, I have been given many opportunities to ponder the extraordinary nature of my life (so far). I'm reminded that we cannot change the system from within and that, instead, we're playing musical chairs on a cruise ship full of systems too entrenched and too overcome with inertia to be altered significantly. I have taken a critical first step, departing from the system before it abandons me. I've stopped feeding the beast, albeit at considerable cost: I am unable to interact regularly with individuals long ignored or marginalized by the main stream.

At the customary end-of-semester meeting of the extended gang of teachers and administrators from *Poetry Inside/Out*, we shared a meal and much laughter, and generally celebrated our latest successes and my contribution to the program as that contribution came to a close. We reflected on one of our first meetings in the county jail, during which one of the men broke down and cried. Considering the strong cultural pressure against crying in contemporary American culture on the outside of prison walls, you can imagine what it's like to show such emotion in jail. Subsequent to that early meeting, raw emotions surfaced many times, and we had an ongoing conversation about crying throughout the entire semester. Initially, an inmate said, "there's no crying in jail." Right away another inmate pointed out that crying was banned from baseball, not jail, as described in the 1992 film, *A League of Their Own*. In the end, we created a superb mix of humor and tragedy, as if jail were a microcosm for society. Which, of course, it is.

Because the *Poetry Inside/Out* conversation extends to an alternative high school and also to the girls' pods in the county detention facility, we have abundant, and abundantly rich, material. Consider, for example, this bit of writing from a 15-year-old girl about to leave detention for a stint in rehab:

My last words, by Little Cloud

Sadly this'll probably be the last time you hear from 'Little Cloud' for those of you who remember me. But I hope the words I've written will have a lasting effect. But this 'sister' can only hope. My last words of advice:

1. We may all be badasses but it's OK to cry
2. Don't give up, it only takes one voice to change the world
3. Even though we are convicts we still are human
4. You are loved, whether you think so or not, us writing to you proves it
5. Listen, for you never know what good you'll hear
6. Make a difference just because you can
7. People will forgive, especially when you think they won't

8. Don't EVER THINK YOU AREN'T WORTH BEING IN THIS WORLD

9. Believe

10. Keep an open mind because doing so will open worlds you never knew

11. How ever long it will be, one way or another you will be free (especially those of you sentenced to life)

12. You aren't stupid, retarded or dumb, those people who say you are, are

13. Don't forget 'Little Cloud' Ha Ha :)

14. We all have the right to grow and change

15. No time is wasted, as long as you feel & really learn

16. Breathe

I'm crying myself, as I type her words. She's fifteen years old and already wiser than I, not to mention just about everybody else I know. I suppose hard times will do that for you.

As we wrapped up our potluck lunch, at the request of my co-teacher and mentor, I read this bit from Pablo Neruda's poem, "Keeping Quiet." It seemed fitting, as I stepped away from the city life to move closer to the land:

For once on the face of the earth
let's not speak in any language,
let's stop for one second,
and not move our arms so much.
It would be an exotic moment
without rush, without engines,
we would all be together
in a sudden strangeness.
Fishermen in the cold sea
would not harm whales
and the man gathering salt
would look at his hurt hands.
Those who prepare green wars,
wars with gas, wars with fire,
victory with no survivors,

would put on clean clothes
and walk about with their brothers
in the shade, doing nothing.
What I want should not be confused
with total inactivity.
Life is what it is about;
I want no truck with death.
If we were not so single-minded
about keeping our lives moving,
and for once could do nothing,
perhaps a huge silence
might interrupt this sadness
of never understanding ourselves
and of threatening ourselves with death.
Perhaps the earth can teach us
as when everything seems dead
and later proves alive.
Now I'll count up to twelve
    and you keep quiet and I will go.

Two views of our future

"The crisis deepens. Everyday life is plundered as much as the physical environment. Our predicament points us toward a solution. The voluntary abandonment of the industrial mode of existence is not self-renunciation, but a healing return."

Thus begins John Zerzan's 2008 manifesto, *Twilight of the Machines*. Those words are, interestingly, placed above the title on the book's cover, which has the author's head-shot photograph taken in a cave. Before turning the first page, the reader knows where this book is headed.

Zerzan is an anarchist, as indicated by the titles of two of his previous books: *Against Civilization* and *Running on Emptiness*. Feral House published both previous books, as well as *Twilight of the Machines*.

Twilight of the Machines begins with a two-page Preface, which includes these lines: "Specialization, domestication, civilization, mass society, modernity, technoculture ... behold Progress, its fruition presented more and more unmistakably. The imperative of control unfolds starkly, pushing us to ask questions equal to the mounting threat around us and within us. These dire times may yet reveal invigorating new vistas of thought and action. When everything is at stake, all must be confronted and superseded. At this moment, there is the distinct possibility of doing just that. ... Clinging to politics is one way to avoid the confrontation with the devouring logic of civilization, holding instead with the accepted assumptions and definitions."

Amen, brother. Seems the direr our situation becomes -- that is, the more we pillage the planet and our fellow human beings -- the more we turn to politics for answers. But there are no political solutions to the crises we face. If there is a politically viable solution to solving global climate change, energy decline, or the nearly complete absence of decent human communities in America, I think we'd have known about it by now.

And yet, the cries continue for Barack Obama, aka Teflon president 2.0, aka the second coming of Ronald Reagan, to save us from ourselves. At this point, we need to push the politicians and the politics out of the way. We need to abandon the system, albeit long after it has abandoned us.

With plenty of supporting citations, *Twilight of the Machines* traces the division of labor to the end of the Paleolithic (i.e., beginning of the Neolithic), coincident with the rise of agriculture and also the rise of organized violence against other humans. Agriculture plants the seeds of war because war is required, for the first time in human history, by agriculture. Once agriculture arrives, bringing with it substantial differences in quality of life for the two sexes, "another dichotomy appears, the distinction between work and non-work, which for so many, many generations did not exist." Echoing his many predecessors, most notably Daniel Quinn, Zerzan interprets the Fall from Eden as a demise of hunter-gatherer life, with its subsequent expulsion into agriculture and hard labor. The victim bears the blame, a common historical pattern.

Shortly after Cain murdered Abel and then founded the first city, more cities began to dot the Mesopotamian landscape. The rewards of civilization allowed relatively few people to feed the majority, with the biggest rewards going to a select, powerful minority. From those days forward, cities have allowed, in Stanley Diamond's words, "conquest abroad and repression at home."

Once the Fall was complete, the battle lines were drawn. Feelings of gratitude toward a freely giving nature were replaced by the ethos of domestication. It's humans against nature, as well as humans against other humans. The resultant top-down, power-based culture gradually led to development of the ultimate top-down, power-based culture. Monotheism conquered the West some two-and-a-half millennia ago.

I think most literate people know the causes and consequences of our dilemmas. There is nothing new in the first half of *Twilight of the Machines*. But Zerzan does a nice job articulating the disaster, yet again. And he does so with relatively few words and also with sufficient evidentiary support to satisfy most skeptics. Similarly, Zerzan offers a way forward in relatively few words: "Primitivists draw strength from their understanding that no matter how bereft our lives have become in the last ten thousand years, for most of our nearly two million years on the planet, human life appears to have been healthy and authentic. ... It's an all or nothing struggle. Anarchy is just a name for those who embrace its promise of redemption and wholeness, and try to face up to how far we'll need to travel to get there. We humans once had it right, if the anthropologists are to be believed. Now we'll find out if we can get it right again. Quite possibly our last opportunity as a species."

I couldn't agree more. It is an all-or-nothing struggle. Continuing along the current path risks our living planet and our species, thus representing simultaneous ecocide and extinction of our own species. (There is no word in the English language for the latter phenomenon, I suppose because suigenocide sounds a bit too German.)

After briefly explaining the messes, and their likely causes, Zerzan calls for a voluntary return to primitivism. I've finally found somebody more optimistic than I am. Whereas I think we'll be riding the post-industrial Stone-Age train quite soon, Zerzan thinks *Homo industrialus* will be fighting, er, bartering, for tickets aboard the train.

I'd love to believe we'll power down with the tranquility of Buddhist monks. But my bet lies elsewhere.

T.C. Boyle's 2000 novel, *A Friend of the Earth*, takes an approach diametrically opposed to *Twilight of the Machines*. The novel describes one man's futile attempts to save the living earth and the consequences of his failure. *A Friend of the Earth* is set in 2025-2026, with frequent flashbacks to 1989 and 1990. In this tale, the industrial age has not reached its end, and the consequences are truly horrific. The effects of habitat loss for many species, along with climate change, have produced a badly overpopulated planet that alternates between madly monsoonal and hellishly hot. The book echoes Jonathan Swift's classic writings from three centuries ago: People are living a long time, relative to today's standards, but their lives are truly miserable.

The novel opens with a quote from Emerson's *Nature* along with one from Tom Waits' song, *Earth Died Screaming*: "The earth died screaming / While I lay dreaming ..." After the opening quotes, we dive right into the miserable existence of Tyrone (Ty) O'Shaughnessy Tierwater, 75-year-old caretaker of the a misbegotten menagerie of nearly extinct animals owned by a wealthy music star still revered years after his glory days.

Clogged with nine billion people trying to eke out a life worth living, the world of 2025 as portrayed by Boyle is simultaneously hauntingly realistic and overly optimistic. The realistic portion concerns the weather: The rainy season in the protagonist's region is comprised of several months in a hurricane, complete with roof-ripping winds and incessant downpours. When the hurricane turns off, the weather promptly switches to achingly arid, with temperatures rarely dipping below 90 F.

I appreciate Boyle's portrayal of the climate and weather in 2025, but I think he is entirely too optimistic about the future of food: It's difficult for me to foresee so many people obtaining enough food to persist well into their second century of life in a world with few remaining species and even fewer remaining forests. When ecosystems collapse to the extent portrayed in *A Friend of the Earth*, you can forget about insect-pollinated plants in the heartland of any continent on this planet.

I'll admit that describing the planet's future, and the role of humans in that presumed future, is a daunting task. Nonetheless, I think James Howard Kunstler's *World Made By Hand* and Cormac McCarthy's *The Road* both offer reasonably plausible scenarios for our prospects in 2025. Ultimately -- and perhaps paradoxically -- both books are more apocalyptic and also more hopeful about our future than *A Friend of the Earth*. On the other hand, Ty's loneliness in a crowded world, induced by his intellect and his passion for the planet, reminds me of an email message I received a few years back from a brilliant former student. It included this pithy line, which expresses, better than I ever have, my oft-felt sentiment: "Despite overpopulation I find the world a lonely place."

There is much to appreciate in Boyle's novel, and not simply due to the reminiscent pleasure of my email in-box. Consider this line as Ty prepares to sabotage a large electrical project in the early 1990s: "All it took was public awareness -- if they only knew what electricity ultimately cost them, if they only knew they were tightening the noose round their own throats, day by day, kilowatt hour by kilowatt hour, then they'd rise up as one and put an end to it." Every thoughtful conservation biologist and friend of the planet knows the feeling and hopes education is sufficient. And yet, by now we all know it isn't working and almost certainly won't.

This brief passage reminds me that novels contain truth deeper than works of non-fiction: "Revenge fantasies got you nowhere. Despair did, though. Despair got you to submit to the gravitational force and become one with the cracked leather couch in front of the eternally blipping TV in a rented house on a palm-lined street in suburbia."

Later, our protagonist reflects on a life in the trenches on behalf the planet's non-human species: "Friendship. That's what got me into the movement and that's what pushed me way out there on the naked edge of nothing, beyond sense or reason, or even hope. Friendship for the earth. For the trees and shrubs and the native grasses and the antelope on the plain and the kangaroo rats in the desert and everything else that lives and breathes under the sun. ... Except people, that is. Because to be a friend of the earth, you have to be an enemy of the people."

Maybe that's why my in-box has all that hate mail. To be fair, though, I would modify the final sentence in the preceding paragraph thusly: "Because to be a friend of the earth, you have to be an enemy of the majority of people in industrialized countries." After all, extant non-industrial cultures and future people will thank friends of the earth for bringing down the industrial economy despite the best efforts of the collective masses who are insanely destroying the planet. Assuming, of course, the industrial economy does not persist through 2025, thereby ensuring there are no future people alive to thank contemporary friends of the earth.

Like Nietzsche, I write for future humans. And, like Nietzsche, my ego allows me to believe future people will appreciate my efforts in ways contemporary humans don't.

Fast forward to Ty's dry season of 2026, driving through northern California: "Of course, there are the inevitable condos. And traffic. This was once a snaking two-lane country road cut through national forest lands, sparsely populated, little-traveled. Now I'm crawling along at fifteen miles an hour in a chain of cars and trucks welded into the flanks of the mountain as far as I can see, and I'm not breathing cooling drafts of alpine air either -- wind-whipped exhaust, that's about it. Where thirty-five years ago there were granite bluffs and domes, now there is stucco and glass and artificial wood, condos banked up atop one another like the Anasazi cliff-dwellings, eyes of glass, teeth of steps and railings, the pumping hearts of air-conditioning units, thousands of them, and no human face in sight. Am I complaining? No. I haven't got the right."

Ouch. Like a knife in my left lung.

Ty struggles until the very end, even as he realizes the futility of his efforts. When asked, in the book's final pages, what he accomplished through passion and hard work that landed him in prison and cost him his health, his marriage, his daughter, and nearly his life, he responds: "Nothing. Absolutely nothing."

Ouch. There goes the other lung.

Friendship, hope, and our post-carbon future

I'm an equal-opportunity offender with a passion for stirring the societal stew. Edward Abbey, the iconoclastic author from Tucson, was fond of saying society is like a stew: if you don't stir it up every now and then, the scum rises to the top. Clearly, we've needed a lot more stirring since we lost Cactus Ed's voice in 1989.

Speaking of scum rising to the top, my dean -- back when I had one -- kept asking me to quit stirring the pot. Apparently by pointing out the absurdities of Americans and their self-indulgent lifestyles, university professors threaten to interrupt the money being siphoned away from big-business donors and toward our football team. So I kept reminding my dean, and anybody else who'd listen, that one of my favorite quotes comes from George Orwell: "If liberty means anything at all, it means the right to tell people what they do not want to hear." Not surprisingly, my dean didn't appreciate Orwell nearly as much as I do. Of course, he didn't appreciate *me* nearly as much as I do, either. Fortunately, if tenure means anything at all, it means the right to tell people what they do not want to hear. In my case, that meant trying to wake people up to a future dominated by economic contraction and ecological destruction. Since a huge number of people seem to be sleeping on the railroad tracks with their earplugs firmly intact, I'm in no danger of running out of people to assail with the big news.

For many years, I have been plagued with the central question underlying Schopenhauer's philosophy: How to get through a life not worth living?

Socrates famously concluded that the unexamined is not worth living. I'm surprised it took two millennia for somebody -- that somebody being Schopenhauer -- to realize that the examined life is far, far worse.

This is one of the many prices we pay for having a PBS mind in an MTV world: We realize that, although ignorance is bliss, bliss is overrated. Otherwise, we'd all be comfortably stoned, all the time.

So then: How to get through a life not worth living?

Schopenhauer gave the answer to his own question in three words: *Will to live*.

Schopenhauer's successor Nietzsche extended this idea with his own three-word answer: *Will to power*. Nietzsche knew the lust for power often exceeds the will to live.

And shortly before his death in 2003, the great human-rights advocate and intellectual leftist Edward Said addressed the issue: "There is no point to intellectual and political work if one were a pessimist. Intellectual and political work require, nay demand, optimism."

Said was suggesting that, without optimism, we may as well take the Hemingway out.

They say the truth will set you free. They lie. The truth does not set you free, it just pisses you off. At least, that's my experience.

I admired Said for his courage, and I still admire his contrarian views. And, as a self-proclaimed intellectual who is often accused of inappropriately meddling in political work, I am naturally inclined toward optimism. There's no reason to stir the pot if you think the human condition is hopeless.

But I suspect Said did not know about peak oil or runaway greenhouse. Surely his optimism would have been dampened, had he only known about these two profound consequences of our insatiable desires.

Oil supply -- at the level of the field, county, state, country, or world -- follows a bell-shaped curve; the top of the curve is called "Peak Oil," or "Hubbert's Peak." We passed Hubbert's Peak for the worldwide extraction of crude oil and began easing down the other side during 2005. Because the United States mainlines cheap oil, it is easy to envision the complete collapse of the U.S. industrial economy within a few years. There is little doubt the entire industrial world will follow suit. The Great Depression will seem like the good old days when unemployment approaches one hundred percent and fiat currency becomes recognized as worthless. Obviously, this is a very good thing for the world's cultures and species, and even for the continued persistence of our own species.

As I wrote in my 2005 book, *Killing the Natives*, "progress" has its price: The problem is not that the road to Hell is paved with good intentions -- it's that the road to Hell is *paved*. We have, to the maximum possible extent allowed by our intellect and never-ending desire, consumed the planet and therefore traded in tomorrow for today. And we keep making these choices, every day, choosing dams over salmon, oil over whales, cars over polar bears, death over life. And when I say we keep making these choices, I do not mean you and me -- we have essentially nothing to do with it -- I mean the politicians and CEOs who run this country. They are killing the planet and, when they notice the screams, they turn up the volume on Fox News. Meanwhile, most Americans took the blue pill from the *Matrix* without really thinking about the consequences. In the wake of these endless insults to our only home, perhaps the biggest surprise is that so many native species have persisted, thus allowing for our continued use and enjoyment.

When I tell people about peak oil, the immediate response is something like, "C'mon, the Dow Jones Industrial Average is cranking up; the economy looks great."

Uh-huh. Never mind the asset bubble built by shaky investments. Never mind the manipulation of the money supply by the Federal Reserve Bank since the Fed's monetary policy was removed from public view by Ben Bernanke. Never mind that the Dow, which is based on a whopping 30 companies, is in free-fall over the last decade when measured against any metric except the U.S. dollar, which is falling even faster. Never mind that serious stock-market investors represent a slim minority of the world's populace.

Ignore all that, and think about this: When you jump off a 100-story building, everything seems fine for a while. In fact, the view just keeps getting clearer as you get closer to the ground. What could possibly go wrong? Well, maybe one thing. It's not the fall that kills you. It's the sudden stop at the bottom.

The American pragmatist philosopher and pacifist William James struggled with the same question every single morning: Shall I get out of bed? I really don't know how he did it. I mean, physically:

Personally, I'm emptying my bladder before I'm fully awake in the morning. So I struggle with the follow-up question: Shall I spend the day teaching and writing, or shall I do something useful? Shall I blow up a freeway, a building, a dam, or some other sign of destruction disguised as progress? (Recognizing that, with my limited practical skills, I'm more likely to blow up myself than a dam.) So far, I've opted for the "civilized" option, the one that results in more people consuming more stuff and hurtling us ever closer to the sudden stop at the bottom of the fall. But tomorrow's a new day; there's hope for me yet. Of course, a career in academia has me ill-prepared for useful work, so I'll have to learn a lot before I can take meaningful action against the machine of death known as western civilization.

Passing Hubbert's Peak may be good news for species and cultures, other than extant humans in industrial culture, but it obviates technological solutions to many of our most pressing problems, including runaway greenhouse. That is, it obviates development of future civilizations. You could argue that technology has never solved a social problem, but only made them worse, so this point may be irrelevant (I would agree with this assessment). If you're a fan of technology, you might conclude that burning the planetary endowment of oil precludes development of a durable civilization on this planet. Any intelligent species that evolves in the wake of our demise -- our planetary successors -- will lack the supply of inexpensive energy necessary to create a durable civilization. Following this line of thought, each planet gets a single shot at "sustainability," and we blew ours when we let the neo-conservatives rip the solar panels off the White House and pursue economic growth as our only god. Again, you could argue -- and I would agree -- that civilization is inherently unsustainable, and that we can approach sustainability only by accelerating civilization's ultimate collapse and forcing us forward into the durable societies of the post-industrial Stone Age.

As the Buddha said, "there is no torrent like greed." Or, as Al Gore said in a pre-election speech about our national energy policy in 2004, this country needs a new dipstick. I did not get the impression he was volunteering. And that's okay with me. I mean, here's a guy who thinks the climate crisis can be solved by a bunch of professional narcissists strutting across the world's stages stroking their Stratocasters. Sorry, folks, but even the world's greatest consumers can't spend our way out of this one.

Speaking of the climate crisis, what about runaway greenhouse? Runaway greenhouse simply means positive feedbacks are overwhelming Earth's climate system and we cannot stop the warming of planet Earth. Had we passed the oil peak a decade earlier, we would have been forced to reduce carbon dioxide emissions and therefore prevent the frying of the planet.

But perhaps peak oil came too late to save us. It appears humanity will be restricted to a few thousand hardy scavengers living near the poles within a few decades. Shortly thereafter, *Homo sapiens* will join, in extinction, every other species to occupy the planet. Recent projections indicate that, before mid-century, there will be no planetary ice. That's dinosaur days, and the end of the human experience. It's very small consolation to me that, as the home team, Nature bats last.

We will persist about ten percent as long as the typical species of mammal, giving credence to Schopenhauer's view that the human experience is a mere blink of an eye bounded on either side by infinities of time. Despite our apparently brief stay on this most wondrous of planets, it has become clear we will take a large percentage of the planet's biological diversity along with us into the abyss.

Alas, "there is no torrent like greed."

Knowledge of peak oil and runaway greenhouse leads me, again, to the question of Schopenhauer: How to get through a life not worth living? I have struggled mightily with this question, and have turned to my intellectual predecessors and heroes for answers.

I start, as I often do, with Socrates. Socrates pursued a life of excellence by questioning those who would tolerate him and his many inquiries. He knew we were beings singularly tuned to quality. In this essay I will mention each of the six primary questions of Socrates, the questions that represent the qualities he found so important to the human condition: What is good? What is piety? What is virtue? What is courage? What is justice? What is moderation? These questions are as vibrant and relevant today as they were more than two millennia ago. For many years, I encouraged my students to consider the questions of Socrates as they attempted to live lives of excellence, and as they moved forward in their promising careers. I suspect many of them were thinking: "My career seemed promising ... until he showed up."

At about the same time Socrates was getting himself killed for asking too many questions, the son of a wealthy king on the other side of the planet was forsaking the family fortune and asking questions of his own. Unlike Socrates, the Buddha was willing to hazard a few answers, which have come to be known as his four noble truths. The first of those truths: "Life is suffering."

It's hard to believe Schopenhauer wasn't a Buddhist, given the primary question underlying his philosophy.

Never mind runaway greenhouse: The Buddha didn't even know about oil, much less peak oil. In the absence of such knowledge the Buddha, like Socrates, concluded that a life of moderation contributes to a life of excellence. I think it's pretty impressive that Socrates and the Buddha reached the very same conclusion even without using the Internet to assist their obvious plagiarism. In the spirit of Socrates and the Buddha, we may want to consider some moderation ourselves, although it's too late for moderation to solve the pressing problems associated with peak oil and runaway greenhouse.

So then, back to the question: How to get through a life not worth living? Schopenhauer was a very smart guy, but his response to his own question is wholly insufficient: Will to live is inadequate for most philosophers, as it is for me.

Nietzsche was perhaps the most brilliant person to occupy the planet so far, but his response similarly leaves me wanting: Will to power is meaningless if we abuse the power, and it seems that abuse of power is what the hairless monkey does best. Small wonder Nietzsche was impressed with Buddhism and the Buddha's second noble truth: "Desire is the source of suffering." As Americans, we expect our every desire to be fulfilled, planet Earth be damned. If our desires include Hummers and hang-gliders, Thai take-out and plasma-screen TVs, well, those are among the many rewards of Empire. As long as the costs of Empire remain obscured from view, we're as happy as pigs in a pile of manure.

So much for these two famous 19th-century German philosophers, Schopenhauer and Nietzsche. But even Said's unremitting optimism may seem unwarranted in light of knowledge that has emerged since his death.

On the other hand, I'm not ready to dismiss Said just yet. My response to the question of Schopenhauer is rooted in Said-style optimism that is perhaps unwarranted but nonetheless undeniable.

You've likely heard the old expression: An optimist believes this is the best of all possible worlds, and a pessimist fears this is true.

My optimistic response to the question of Schopenhauer has two primary components: friendship and hope.

I'll talk a little more about hope shortly. But I'll start with friendship.

I turn to Aristotle for my favorite definition of friendship: a relationship between people working together on a project for the common good. Without the common good, we might as well restrict friendship to drinking buddies. The distinction is as clear as that between being a *citizen* and being a *consumer*. Sadly, I suspect most Americans don't know the difference.

In Aristotle's definition of friendship we find traces of his teacher's teacher, Socrates. After all, one of Socrates' six primary questions was, "What is good?" For focusing on the common good, I suspect Socrates would have been pleased with Aristotle, and perhaps even with those of us committed to saving our species, although I will admit it may be asking too much to expect the blessing of a long-dead Greek Cynic.

And speaking of Greek Cynics, it's pretty clear the prophet of America's dominant religion was heavily influenced by Greeks and especially the Cynics. Yet a *Time* magazine poll conducted in 2006 found that more than three in five Christians in the United States believe God wants them to be financially prosperous. Never mind the biblical root of all evil. Never mind the gospels, especially the gospel of Mark. When three out of five self-proclaimed followers of a poor, homeless prophet who dedicated his life to working with the poor believe they are entitled to wealth, it's no wonder you don't hear much about the common good these days. This stunning statistic brings to mind another of Socrates' questions: "What is piety?"

The *Greatest Generation* of Tom Brokaw, the generation that saved the world from fascism during World War II -- or so the story goes -- that's the generation that begat the greatest generation of consumers in world history. It's been a wild ride, but it's time to turn out the lights: The party's just about over. The baby-boom generation's legacy, their "gift" to all of us, is a world depleted of fossil fuels, soil, water, and healthy landbases, ruined by Empire, and ruled by fascism masquerading as Republic.

In *One with Nineveh*, ecologists Paul and Anne Ehrlich describe the American social system as, "capitalism for the poor, socialism for the rich." Our socioeconomic system is designed to subsidize the wealthy and pulverize the downtrodden. And also, of course, to pulverize our precious resources.

Contrary to society's general disregard for the common good, I have to believe that the greatest measure of our humanity is found in what we do for those who cannot take care of themselves: the myriad species, cultures, and yes, even impoverished individuals in our own country, who never stood a chance in the face of American-style capitalism.

I have to believe, in other words, that our humanity is measured in our willingness to protect the common good. And, by pursuing and protecting the common good, we become friends in the Aristotelian sense.

I'm willing to call the pursuit of the common good an exercise in virtue, bringing to mind another Socratic question: "What is virtue?"

By focusing on alleviation of suffering and the persistence of our species, we may be pursuing the common good. But I will be the first to admit that we have our differences. Indeed, the wonder of DNA ensures our uniqueness. The odds against any one of us being here are greater than the odds against being a particular grain of sand on all the world's beaches. In fact, the odds are much greater than that: they exceed the odds of being a single atom plucked from the entire universe. To quote the evolutionary biologist Richard Dawkins, "In the teeth of these stupefying odds it is you and I that are privileged to be here, privileged with eyes to see where we are and brains to wonder why." If a student in one of my classes wrote like that, I would reward the sentiment while correcting the grammar.

That's enough about friendship for now. What about hope, the second component of my optimistic response to Schopenhauer's question?

I view hope as the left-brain product of love, analogous to democracy as the product of freedom, or liberty. Notably, Patrick Henry did not say, "Give me democracy or give me death." Like the rest of the founding fathers, Henry knew that freedom was primary to democracy; without the guiding light of freedom, or liberty, democracy breaks up on the shoals. Love keeps our left brain in check -- that's the message of the world's religions. But our right-brain love creates the foundation for hope: love for nature, love for our children and grandchildren, love for each other. Without love to light the way, hope breaks up on the shoals.

Mind you, hope is not simply wishful thinking. And that's a problem, considering we're immersed in the ultimate "wishful thinking, something-for-nothing" culture. How else to explain books such as *The Secret*, which proclaims that happy thoughts will generate happy results, including personal wealth? How else to explain the prevalence of, and widespread acceptance of, casinos and state-sponsored lotteries? And it's not just acceptance: it's adoration, if the boob tube and the local movie theater are to be believed. Not so long ago, gambling was frowned upon because, instead of adhering to a culture of an honest day's pay for an honest day's work, it reflects the expectation that a person can get something for nothing. No, hope is not wishful thinking.

And another thing: hope is not a consumer product. You can't walk into Wal-Mart and order up a carton of hope. Indeed, given the demise of cheap oil, there's unlikely to be a Wal-Mart -- or any other large institution, for that matter -- to walk into at all within a few years. Even if Wal-Mart, the federal government, or our universities somehow find a way to survive, we're going to have to generate our own hope, one person at a time. Just as an economic collapse happens one person at a time, so too must hope happen one person at a time.

When I'm not playing social critic, I am a conservation biologist. I admit conservation biology is a value-laden enterprise, hampered by, and perhaps assisted by, bridges between the left and right hemispheres of the brain. The greatest value of Earth is, always has been, and always will be, that it exists. Not that it is useful. But that it is. Perhaps that makes me an artist trapped in a scientific pursuit. But, at least for me, it allows hope to emerge from the tonic of wildness, thereby providing context for this most insignificant of lives. It allows hope to flicker. And if there is a flicker of hope, I believe we must treat it like a beacon. Hope, my friends, is everywhere.

"Hope is the thing with feathers," said Emily Dickinson. Her other poems indicate that she was not restricting her thoughts to birds: Dickinson found hope throughout the glory and wonder of nature.

My friend and colleague, the planner Vern Swaback, is fond of saying he finds hope in "a person's dedicated life." I cannot improve upon Vern's comment, but I can offer a few other personal examples.

I find hope in the poems of the teenaged girls at the juvenile detention facility where I helped teach stewardship through poetry. And also in the poems of the men in jail, with whom the girls shared their poetry.

And I could see hope flickering every day in the eyes -- and therefore in the minds and in the hearts -- of the students with whom I was fortunate to work on a daily basis.

Hope is our humility overcoming our hubris in the face of long odds. This will require an enormous amount of courage. We must rise to Nietzschean heights in the style of the Overman.

Hope is self-proclaimed liberals and self-proclaimed conservatives in the same room, discussing our common future.

Hope, then, rooted in friendship, is my response to Schopenhauer. Hope, in other words, rooted in friendship -- let's call it Platonic love -- rooted in the right-brained friendship expressed by honoring each other and hugging trees.

Will to live is no solution: It's a problem, as Schopenhauer himself admitted when he proclaimed, "to desire immortality is to desire the eternal perpetuation of a great mistake."

Our will to live, rooted in the evolutionary drive to survive, makes us shortsighted and self-motivated (or, in the case of many of us, self-absorbed).

We are inherently incapable of considering, much less empathizing with, our grandchildren's grandchildren. That's why we are willing to bake the planet beyond the point of habitability within a very few generations. This brings to mind another question of Socrates: "What is justice?" I do not know what justice is, but I know it is unjust to leave the world worse than we found it.

It seems evolution dealt us a bad hand. It gave us the big brains, but they're not quite big enough.

Evolution drives us toward "flight or fight" -- that is, to survival.

If we survive, evolution drives us to procreate: Nearly four billion years of evolution by natural selection are screaming at us to breed. Evolution has some bad company on this one, in the form of the world's largest religious group, and the world's fastest-growing one.

If we clear the first two hurdles, evolution prods us to acquire material possessions.

And these three outcomes of evolution -- the drives to live, procreate, and accumulate possessions -- are disastrous to the common good.

If Schopenhauer's "will to live" offers no viable solution, Nietzsche's "will to power" is even worse, for it reveals our darkest nature. It's small wonder Nietzsche abandoned the Overman late in his career. Or perhaps the Overman abandoned Nietzsche.

Maybe Said wasn't so far off the mark:

Said said "optimism." I say "hope."

Said said "intellectual and political work." I say "the common good."

But we seem not so far apart, Said and I. Just like, on close inspection, those of us committed to alleviating suffering and extending the persistence of our species on the planet: Our intellectual and political

211

work require, nay demand, optimism. For without it, hope is lost for both kinds of humanity:

Without optimism, hope is lost for the individual, personal variety of humanity that is the measure of our character.

And without optimism, hope is lost for our entire species, and many others on this planet. That hope is lost, too, without big doses of courage, justice, moderation, and virtue.

How do we get from here to there? How do we, in the words of the anthropologist and poet Loren Eiseley, "seek a minor sun" when faced with our final freezing battle with the void? How do we, as a species, use our hope and our friendship to address the urgent issue of peak oil while simultaneously solving the problem of runaway greenhouse? These are the greatest challenges humanity has ever faced. Tackling either of them, without the loss of a huge number of human lives, will require tremendous courage, compassion, and creativity. Many experts who write about simply one of these issues -- peak oil -- predict collapse of the world's industrial economy within a few years, followed shortly thereafter by utter chaos and the subsequent death of more than four-fifths of the world's population. After all, the exponential curve of human population growth matches perfectly the exponential growth of world energy supply, suggesting that the downturn of the energy curve will cause a large-scale die-off of human beings. And if you think chaos can't descend on this country, you weren't paying attention to New Orleans in the wake of hurricane Katrina. Horrible as that event was, nearly everybody involved knew it was a temporary inconvenience; I'm concerned how people might act when they recognize peak oil as a long emergency. One by one, the world's cities will experience permanent blackouts; and once we enter the Dark Age, the post-industrial Stone Age won't be too far behind. Bear in mind, I have mixed feelings about this. On one hand, I know the current culture -- the culture of make believe, or the culture of death, depending on how deeply you care to think about it -- is the worst possible route for most of the planet's species; as a conservation biologist, I realize the faster and more complete the collapse of Empire, the greater our biological legacy and the better chance we have of persisting as a species beyond mid-century. On the other hand, the paralyzing hand of fear grips me every time I think about peak oil; a life in the ivory tower is damned poor preparation for Stone-Age living. Fortunately, I only think about it a few thousand times each day.

Can we get from here to there? We have the best excuse in the world to not act. The momentum of civilization is powerful. Resisting those in power will almost certainly lead to imprisonment, torture, perhaps even death. Those are pretty good excuses to forego action. So the question becomes, in the words of author and activist Derrick Jensen: "Would you rather have the best excuse in the world, or would you rather have a world?" To tackle peak oil and runaway greenhouse at the same time might require larger doses of courage, compassion, and creativity than we can find in ourselves.

But I hope not. And in that hope, I turn to the premises behind Derrick Jensen's 2007 masterpiece, *Endgame*. May they guide us beyond the greed of the industrial age and into the post-industrial Stone Age.

Premise One: Civilization is not and can never be sustainable. This is especially true for industrial civilization.

Premise Two: Traditional communities do not often voluntarily give up or sell the resources on which their communities are based until their communities have been destroyed. They also do not willingly allow their landbases to be damaged so that other resources -- gold, oil, and so on -- can be extracted. It follows that those who want the resources will do what they can to destroy traditional communities.

Premise Three: Our way of living -- industrial civilization -- is based on, requires, and would collapse very quickly without persistent and widespread violence.

Premise Four: Civilization is based on a clearly defined and widely accepted yet often unarticulated hierarchy. Violence done by those higher on the hierarchy to those lower is nearly always invisible, that is, unnoticed. When it is noticed, it is fully rationalized. Violence done by those lower on the hierarchy to those higher is unthinkable, and when it does occur is regarded with shock, horror, and the fetishization of the victims.

Premise Five: The property of those higher on the hierarchy is more valuable than the lives of those below. It is acceptable for those above to increase the amount of property they control -- in everyday language, to make money -- by destroying or taking the lives of those below. This is called production. If those below damage the property of those above, those above may kill or otherwise destroy the lives of those below. This is called justice.

Premise Six: Civilization is not redeemable. This culture will not undergo any sort of voluntary transformation to a sane and sustainable way of living. If we do not put a halt to it, civilization will continue to immiserate the vast majority of humans and to degrade the planet until it (civilization, and probably the planet) collapses. The effects of this degradation will continue to harm humans and nonhumans for a very long time.

Premise Seven: The longer we wait for civilization to crash -- or the longer we wait before we ourselves bring it down -- the messier will be the crash, and the worse things will be for those humans and nonhumans who live during it, and for those who come after.

Premise Eight: The needs of the natural world are more important than the needs of the economic system.

Another way to put premise Eight: Any economic or social system that does not benefit the natural communities on which it is based is unsustainable, immoral, and stupid. Sustainability, morality, and intelligence (as well as justice) requires the dismantling of any such economic or social system, or at the very least disallowing it from damaging your landbase.

Premise Nine: Although there will clearly some day be far fewer humans than there are at present, there are many ways this reduction in population could occur (or be achieved, depending on the passivity or activity with which we choose to approach this transformation). Some of these ways would be characterized by extreme violence and privation: nuclear armageddon, for example, would reduce both population and consumption, yet do so horrifically; the same would be true for a continuation of overshoot, followed by crash. Other ways could be characterized by less violence. Given the current levels of violence by this culture against both humans and the natural world, however, it's not possible to speak of reductions in population and consumption that do not involve violence and privation, not because the reductions themselves would necessarily involve violence, but because violence and privation have become the default. Yet some ways of reducing population and consumption, while still violent, would consist of decreasing the current levels of violence required, and caused by, the (often forced) movement of resources from the poor to the rich, and would of course be marked by a reduction in current violence against the natural world. Personally and collectively we may be able to both reduce the amount and soften the character of violence that occurs during this ongoing and perhaps long-term shift. Or we may not. But this much is certain: if we do not approach it actively -- if we do not talk about our predicament and what we are going to do about it -- the violence will almost undoubtedly be far more severe, the privation more extreme.

Premise Ten: The culture as a whole and most of its members are insane. The culture is driven by a death urge, an urge to destroy life.

Premise Eleven: From the beginning, this culture -- civilization -- has been a culture of occupation.

Premise Twelve: There are no rich people in the world, and there are no poor people. There are just people. The rich may have lots of pieces of green paper that many pretend are worth something -- or their presumed riches may be even more abstract: numbers on hard drives at banks -- and the poor may not. These "rich" claim they own land, and the "poor" are often denied the right to make that same claim. A primary purpose of the police is to enforce the delusions of those with lots of pieces of green paper. Those without the green papers generally buy into these delusions almost as quickly and completely as those with. These delusions carry with them extreme consequences in the real world.

Premise Thirteen: Those in power rule by force, and the sooner we break ourselves of illusions to the contrary, the sooner we can at least begin to make reasonable decisions about whether, when, and how we are going to resist.

Premise Fourteen: From birth on -- and probably from conception, but I'm not sure how I'd make the case -- we are individually and collectively enculturated to hate life, hate the natural world, hate the wild, hate wild animals, hate women, hate children, hate our bodies, hate and fear our emotions, hate ourselves. If we did not hate the world, we could not allow it to be destroyed before our eyes. If we did not hate ourselves, we could not allow our homes -- and our bodies -- to be poisoned.

Premise Fifteen: Love does not imply pacifism.

Premise Sixteen: The material world is primary. This does not mean that the spirit does not exist, nor that the material world is all there is. It means that spirit mixes with flesh. It means also that real-world actions have real-world consequences. It means we cannot rely on Jesus, Santa Claus, the Great Mother, or even the Easter Bunny to get us out of this mess. It means this mess really is a mess, and not just the movement of God's eyebrows. It means we have to face this mess ourselves. It means that for the time we are here on Earth -- whether or not we end up somewhere else after we die, and whether we are condemned or privileged to live here -- the Earth is the point. It is primary. It is our home. It is everything. It is silly to think or act or be as though this world is not real and primary. It is silly and pathetic to not live our lives as though our lives are real.

Premise Seventeen: It is a mistake (or more likely, denial) to base our decisions on whether actions arising from these will or won't frighten fence-sitters, or the mass of Americans.

Premise Eighteen: Our current sense of self is no more sustainable than our current use of energy or technology.

Premise Nineteen: The culture's problem lies above all in the belief that controlling and abusing the natural world is justifiable.

Premise Twenty: Within this culture, economics -- not community well-being, not morals, not ethics, not justice, not life itself -- drives social decisions.

Modification of Premise Twenty: Social decisions are determined primarily (and often exclusively) on the basis of whether these decisions will increase the monetary fortunes of the decision-makers and those they serve.

Re-modification of Premise Twenty: Social decisions are determined primarily (and often exclusively) on the basis of whether these decisions will increase the power of the decision-makers and those they serve.

Re-modification of Premise Twenty: Social decisions are founded primarily (and often exclusively) on the almost entirely unexamined belief that the decision-makers and those they serve are entitled to magnify their power and/or financial fortunes at the expense of those below.

Re-modification of Premise Twenty: If you dig to the heart of it -- if there were any heart left -- you would find that social decisions are determined primarily on the basis of how well these decisions serve the ends of controlling or destroying wild nature.

This, then, is the bottom line: This is not the time for wishful thinking. It's the time for doing. The way to feel hopeful about the future is to get off your butt and demonstrate to yourself, and perhaps to others, that you are a capable, competent individual determinedly able to face new circumstances.

I'll finish this essay where I started, which was the common good as the basis for friendship and hope. And, of course, with the ancients.

Without the common good, and the struggle on its behalf, there can be no Aristotelian friendship. There can be no justice. And there can be no virtue.

Therefore, I am forced to conclude that: Several thousand generations into the human experience, with the end of humanity in clear view, our shared goal must be the common good.

And I further conclude that: As friends, we reveal our differences, we appreciate our differences, and then we set them aside, for the common good.

With hope shining like a beacon, we struggle together, for the common good.

We have in our hands the destiny of our planet, including our own species and so many others. In the end, for finite beings such as ourselves, the historical process is irrelevant; all we have is our legacy, but that legacy is lost to us (as individuals). Yet we are unique beings in that we are able to recognize the historical process as something larger than ourselves. We judge that process worthy or not worthy based on our own singular experience (we judge the universe; fortunately, it doesn't judge us back). For me, the universe is a worthy endeavor because the lens through which I view it is colored with the relationships I have experienced; those relationships include humans and nature.

All the Socratic ideals are born again in the love we feel ... for each other, for our families and tribes, and for the natural world. Walking a path that honors the planet and ourselves is a responsibility we share, you and I -- a responsibility unlike any other in human history. And it is not just a responsibility, but also something more: It is a joy, and a privilege.

Humanity at a crossroads

The evidence is gaining increasing clarity: We've reached a crossroads unlike any other in human history. One path leads to despair for *Homo industrialis*. The other leads to extinction, for *Homo sapiens* and the millions of species we are taking with us into the abyss. I'll take door number one.

I'm reminded of the three Chinese curses.

May you live in interesting times

Mission accomplished. I'm there, as we all are. As we always have been, during two million years of the human experience.

May you attract the attention of the government

I'm there, as I have been for years. To remove all doubt, more than five years ago I placed a call to then-Governor Janet Napolitano's lead advisors on two topics, Energy, and Agriculture & Natural Resources. I begged and pleaded with them, but they kept coming back with their singular response: "There is nothing we can do about global peak oil."

It took a couple years for me to figure out what they meant because, of course, there are many things the government can and should do to mitigate for declining energy supplies. Government officials could start by letting citizens in on the truth about energy.

So, what did members of the governor's staff really mean? There are no politically viable solutions. In this case, telling the truth is political suicide. The impending death of millions of people -- and perhaps billions -- pales in comparison to political careerism.

May you find what you're looking for
I'm talking to a naturalist I barely know. His one-year-old son is resting on his shoulders and treating a cattail as his personal magic wand. The seeds of the cattail are falling into the hair and beard of the 40-year-old naturalist as the boy succumbs to his own personal energy crisis and, fighting all the way down, succumbs to slumber.

I'm writing a book about the dire nature of our predicaments and I mention the high likelihood of a global economic collapse within a decade or so. The naturalist doesn't bat an eye before responding: "I hope I'm around to see it. I don't want my son to have all the fun."

Fast forward seven years, and I'm sharing a property with the naturalist and his young son. Collapse of the industrial economy is well underway, and has entered the acceleration phase of its death spiral. Obviously, we will live to see the final stages of the ongoing collapse of the industrial economy. As a result, we might see the living planet take the first tentative steps to a comeback.

Or perhaps not. Maybe in the coming few years we will die, collateral damage of the demise of the industrial economy. Just like entire ecosystems in the Gulf of Mexico and the millions of organisms within them as oil overwhelms them, consumed by the fire of industrialization as Rome goes up in flames.

Maybe lifting the curse of industry will reveal a worse fate, at least at the level of individuals. But it's difficult to imagine a situation in which termination of the industrial age will not improve the lots of every non-industrial culture and every non-human species on this planet.

May we find what we're looking for, regardless of the personal cost.

Fortunately, the path of despair for *Homo industrialis* gives us one final chance to rescue humanity. And I'm not considering merely our own species. Consider, for example, these definitions from the *Merriam-Webster Dictionary*:

1: the quality or state of being humane (i.e., marked by compassion, sympathy, or consideration for humans or animals)

2 **a**: the quality or state of being human **b**: plural: human attributes or qualities

3: plural: the branches of learning (as philosophy, arts, or languages) that investigate human constructs and concerns as opposed to natural processes (as in physics or chemistry) and social relations (as in anthropology or economics)

4: the human race: the totality of human beings

Sure, that fourth definition matters. We're selfish creatures, after all, interested primarily in our persistence. Unfortunately for our species, we're really, truly interested in persistence of our own selfish selves, and not so much interested in our own species. Ergo, the self-induced, greed-inspired, utterly human, generally predictable (but specifically chaotic) predicaments in which we are currently marinating.

As a society, we will not willingly halt the industrial economy. We would much rather reduce the planet to a lifeless pile of rubble than diminish -- much less halt -- economic growth. But, soon enough, we'll run out of options and the industrial economy will take its last breath, thereby giving us our final, slim hope for averting extinction within the next few decades.

But I'd like to consider the other three definitions, too. If we're to bring down the industrial economy, and therefore save our own sorry asses from our own self-induced, greed-inspired, ... well, you know ... then we're going to have to tap deeply and meaningfully into definitions one, two, and three. In so doing, we just might retain the attributes associated with definitions one, two, and three. But only if we get serious about throwing large buckets of sand into the economic gears of empire.

We could argue all day about the first definition (the others, too, for that matter). Are we capable of being humane? How deeply do you have to drill into your memory to come up with a time you saw a large group of people acting compassionately, sympathetically, considerately toward other humans or animals? On the other hand -- and please excuse my eternally optimistic outlook as it bubbles to the surface yet again -- it's probably quite easy to recall the last time you saw an individual human being displaying those same characteristics. Probably it was you, earlier today.

There's plenty of evolutionary theory to explain altruism among individuals in small groups, even if the individuals do not share grandparents. That same evolutionary theory becomes tenuous, verging on useless, when group size becomes sufficiently large. Throw in all the attributes of industrial culture, nearly all of which reward competition and individualism over cooperation and teamwork, and suddenly we're trapped beneath an avalanche of self-generated hubris.

If we manage to retain the quality or state of being humane -- that is, if we are to retain some semblance of compassion, sympathy, or consideration for humans or animals -- we must jump off the imperial train before it crashes in a heap at the bottom of the precipitous fall. There is some question about whether the train has driven off the cliff, but there can be no doubt it left the station quite a while ago. There is no legitimate hope for saving the industrial economy or a large proportion of the nearly seven billion humans on Earth, but there is great hope for saving the "quality or state of being humane" for relatively small groups of humans.

Will you be part of one of those groups? Will you be among the people with access to water, food, shelter, and a decent human community?

On, then, to the second definition: the quality or state of being human. What makes us human? The question is, of course, easy to address on the surface and nearly impossible to address in depth.

DNA tells us whether we're human, that is, whether we're of the genus *Homo* and the species *Homo sapiens*, as opposed to one of the myriad other organisms on the planet. We'll leave the easy question to gene jockeys, and take up the more difficult and deeper question: What makes us human, beyond DNA?

I'm hardly the first person to ponder that question. My predecessors include a recent special issue of *Nature* (Great Britain's preeminent scientific journal), Hollywood, British television, and dozens of authors, including a passel of philosophers dating at least to Plato and Lao Tzu. I defer, as I often do, to Nietzsche (particularly in *Human, All Too Human*). Nietzsche recognized humans as tragically flawed organisms that, like other animals, lack free will. Unlike Descartes, Nietzsche thought our flaws define us, and therefore cannot be overcome. We are far too human for that. Although we are thinking animals -- what Nietzsche termed res cogitans -- we are prey to muddled thoughts, that is, to ideas that lack clarity and distinctness. Nietzsche wasn't so pessimistic or naive to believe all our thoughts are muddled, of course. Ultimately, though, incompetence defines the human experience.

It's a short, easy step from Nietzsche's conclusion -- we are flawed organisms -- to industrial culture as a product of our incompetence. But the same step can be taken for every technology, with industrial culture as the potentially fatal blow. In other words, progress means only that we accelerate the rapidity with which bad things happen to societies. American exceptionalism thus becomes one more victim of the imperial train wreck.

If this second definition of humanity contributed to the tragedy of industrial culture -- and it's difficult for me to believe it didn't -- is it, like definition number one, worth saving? Will completion of the ongoing industrial collapse retain our inherent, all-too-human flaw?

This question is analogous to John Stuart Mill's famous line from *Utilitarianism*: "It is better to be a human being dissatisfied than a pig satisfied." We simply don't have a choice in the matter (and neither did Mill's pig). We're tragically flawed regardless of the industrial economy's lifespan. In this case, bringing down civilization neither benefits nor harms our humanity.

The third definition of humanity: "the branches of learning (as philosophy, arts, or languages) that investigate human constructs and concerns as opposed to natural processes (as in physics or chemistry) and social relations (as in anthropology or economics)." The branches of learning are defined by the culture. In the present case, arbitrarily dividing knowledge into natural sciences and the humanities has contributed to the division we see at all levels of human interaction. Echoing C.P. Snow's conclusion in his eponymous essay on our two cultures, Edward O. Wilson's argued forcefully in *Consilience* that the separation of learning, hence knowledge, into two groups is a huge blow to meaningfully understanding the human experience. C.P. Snow was, of course, echoing Plato and Lao Tzu.

Shouldn't we be trying to integrate knowledge, instead of compartmentalizing it? In an effort to serve the culture of death that is industrial society, we have taken the worst possible approach: We developed our entire educational system around the twin pillars of compartmentalization and ignorance. Throw in a huge, ongoing, forceful dose of opposition to integration and synthesis, and we're left with a tsunami of incompetence. We probably stood no chance of overcoming the all-too-human incompetence described by Nietzsche, but we purposely designed an educational system to reinforce the incompetence on a massive scale. Is it any wonder, to steal a line from writer and social critic James Howard Kunstler, we're a nation of overfed clowns?

It's easy to blame industrial culture for the sorry state of our educational system, and therefore for our lack of relevant humanity. But I think it's an equally easy path toward improving education by terminating industrial culture. A truly comprehensive approach to learning would focus on humans as *part of* the world, rather than *apart from* the world. It would strive for integration and synthesis. It would assume the learner is one part of an ecosystem, but not a superior part. It would be as unique to a specific location as climate, topography, and the durable culture that assumes its place in that place. In a single semester, two undergraduate students put together just such a curriculum working with me on an independent-study project.

About that fourth and final definition, the one that absorbs our tender existential psyches: Nobody who ever gave the matter serious thought could honestly reach the conclusion that "the totality of human beings" was destined to last forever. But we would try to bring down industrial civilization if we had even a token amount of "compassion, sympathy, or consideration for humans or animals." Our persistent, ridiculous, and all-too-human attempts to prop up the industrial economy not only reveal our stunning lack of humanity, they pose a grave threat to our species.

Humanity is at a crossroads. Let's save it, shall we?

When I write or speak about global climate change or energy decline -- and often I do both, in the same session -- I am often accused of "being negative." My friends and colleagues keep calling on me to lighten up.

The vast majority of people in the world still do not know about the most important issues in the history of our species. Apparently they prefer to remain ignorant. Not only do they not know what's coming, they don't want to know.

These are interesting times for lightening up. Every bit of news about the industrial economy -- shockingly to neoclassical economists -- is dire and growing worse. The stimulus money has run out, but there's more on the way. The Greatest Depression is proceeding apace, and even the mainstream media have begun to notice the rapidity with which things are falling apart between never-ending worship of their heroes in the fields of athletics and cinema, occasionally mixed with a story about somebody shooting somebody else on an overshot planet. Our immorality has insulted the living planet nearly to the point of complete environmental collapse and my readers are worried I will insult somebody about to toss yet another Molotov cocktail into the living, breathing web on which we all depend for our existence. I wouldn't be surprised at chaos in the streets of every industrial nation within a matter of months as the economy implodes, and there is no doubt we will continue to foul the air, dirty the waters, and generally destroy every aspect of our planetary life-support system, so it's difficult for me to understand the rationale behind toning down the message about collapse of the industrial economy.

But, according to my email in-box, I'm about as sharp as a marble. So there's a decent chance I'm merely clueless.

If you're into that kind of thing, it's hardly the time for thinking about making other arrangements. If you haven't made the all-important first step of adjusting your outlook about the future, you're about to become fodder for detritivores. It's time for action, not sitting on your gluteus maximi, pontificating. If you're still thinking about which seat to occupy before the movie starts, here's a clue: the smoke you smell and the flames you see are not part of tonight's film. The people pointing out the fire in the theater are not extras.

Others are being assailed to lighten up, too, if my email in-box is to be believed. After a little thought, I have a couple responses. Feel free to use them on your friends.

With respect to global climate change, the facts are depressing. The only way around this reality is denial, so I understand why so many people spend so much time there. But for rationalists, the burden of reality is shouldered as one consequence of reason. In short, we're stuck with horrible facts on the climate-change front. However, I have a solution, as I am happy to point out: Terminating the industrial economy might allow the continued persistence of our species and many others. This tidbit of good news -- the only solution, to my knowledge, to the global-change predicament -- does not instantly convert listeners to my version of happy-talk optimism. This leads to the second side of the fossil-fuel coin, the one on which I'm deemed particularly negative.

The statement, "the end of cheap oil means the end of the industrial economy" is viewed as negative. My initial response requires no passion, except for passion about facts. Any rational person can be convinced of the following facts: (1) We passed the world peak in extraction of crude oil several years ago, according to abundant evidence arising from models and data; (2) spikes in the price of crude oil have preceded all six global economic recessions since 1972, with bigger spikes preceding deeper economic recessions; (3) the world's industrial economy requires abundant supplies of inexpensive crude oil; (4) there is no politically viable solution to energy decline; and (5) civilizations fall, doubtless including this one. These facts, which are not exactly rooted in faith-based junk science, do not make me pessimistic. Quite to the contrary, they give me great hope for our future. If these facts make you unhappy, or if they make you think I am stuck in negativity, I think this says more about you than it does about me. That is, if you view the facts as negative -- and I don't -- I think that makes you, not me, a purveyor of negativity.

I agree we are headed for a future with fewer luxuries and fewer people. And this poses perhaps the greatest challenge we have faced as a species: Can we muster the creativity, courage, and compassion to see the living world make a comeback? And more importantly, *will* we?

I won't even bother pursuing the issue of morality. Anybody who has given a moment's thought to the issue recognizes the industrial economy is immoral. We have a moral imperative to terminate the industrial economy, the apex of which is city living. But nobody views himself as immoral, regardless of where or how he lives, so the moral imperative is ignored, along with the common good, in pursuit of contemporary conveniences for imperialists in denial.

My second and more obvious response to our peak-oil predicament takes us back four paragraphs: To my knowledge, only completion of the ongoing collapse of the industrial economy collapse saves the living planet upon which we depend for our lives. To my knowledge, only completion of the ongoing collapse of the industrial economy saves our species from runaway greenhouse. To my knowledge, only completion of the ongoing collapse of the industrial economy allows us to retain our humanity. What's not to like about that? And what's so negative about it?

CPSIA information can be obtained at www.ICGtesting.com
Printed in the USA
LVOW071827170412

277996LV00006B/31/P